Insights You Need from
Harvard Business Review

CORONAVIRUS + BUSINESS

We launched the Insights Series to provide our readers with HBR's latest thinking on the future of business—we never foresaw a topic that would have such a sudden and severe impact on business and society and as a whole.

This accelerated print edition of *Coronavirus and Business: The Insights You Need from Harvard Business Review* is a compilation of 16 recent articles from HBR.org. It provides you with essential thinking about keeping your company running remotely, managing your business through disaster and recovery, and finding it within yourself to lead with resilience through the crisis.

HBR is dedicated to helping companies, managers, and others make sense of this uncertain situation. We will continue to publish new articles on coronavirus and business each day, free for all readers, at hbr.org/coronavirus.

Harvard Business Review

Business is changing.
Will you adapt or be left behind?

Get up to speed and deepen your understanding of the topics that are shaping your company's future with the **Insights You Need from Harvard Business Review** series. Featuring HBR's smartest thinking on fast-moving issues—blockchain, cybersecurity, AI, and more—each book provides the foundational introduction and practical case studies your organization needs to compete today, and collects the best research, interviews, and analysis to get it ready for tomorrow.

You can't afford to ignore how these issues will transform the landscape of business and society. The **Insights You Need** series will help you grasp these critical ideas— and prepare you and your company for the future.

THE TITLES INCLUDE:

Available on hbr.org/insights

Harvard Business Review Press Quantity Sales Discounts

Harvard Business Review Press titles are available at significant quantity discounts when purchased in bulk for client gifts, sales promotions, and premiums. Special editions, including books with corporate logos, customized covers, and letters from the company or CEO printed in the front matter, as well as excerpts of existing books, can also be created in large quantities for special needs.

For details and discount information for both print and ebook formats, contact booksales@harvardbusiness.org, tel. 800-988-0886, or www.hbr.org/bulksales.

The web addresses referenced in this book were live and correct at the time of the book's publication but may be subject to change.

Cataloging-in-Publication data is forthcoming.

ISBN: 9781647820466

Contents

SECTION 1
MANAGING YOUR BUSINESS

Harvard Business Review

CRISIS MANAGEMENT

Lead Your Business Through the Coronavirus Crisis

by Martin Reeves, Nikolaus Lang and Philipp Carlsson-Szlezak

FEBRUARY 27, 2020

ABABIL12/GETTY IMAGES

The Covid-19 crisis has now reached a new critical phase where public health systems need to act decisively to contain the growth in new epicenters outside China.

Clearly, the main emphasis is and should be on containing and mitigating the disease itself. But the economic impacts are also significant, and many companies are feeling their way towards understanding, reacting to, and learning lessons from rapidly unfolding events. Unanticipated twists and turns will be revealed with each news cycle, and we will only have a complete picture in retrospect.

Nevertheless, given the very different degrees of preparedness across companies, the further potential for disruption, and the value of being better prepared for future crises, it's worth trying to extract what we have learned so far. Based on our ongoing analysis and support for our clients around the world, we have distilled the following 12 lessons for responding to unfolding events, communicating, and extracting and applying learnings.

1) Update intelligence on a daily basis.

Events are unfolding with astounding speed, and the picture changes on a daily basis. Only several days ago, it looked like the outbreak was mostly confined to China and was being brought under control. More recently, a number of fast-growing epicenters of infection have sprung up beyond China, signaling a new phase and potentially necessitating new strategies of mitigation rather than containment. Our team initially decided to communicate updates every 72 hours, but we moved to a daily cycle, not only for updating data, but also for reframing our overall perspective.

2) Beware of hype cycles / news cycles.

News organizations often focus on what's new rather than the big picture, and they sometimes don't distinguish between hard facts, soft facts, and speculation. Yesterday's news is likely to frame how your organization thinks about the crisis today. When exposed to fast changing information, be it a new technology or an emerging crisis, we have a systematic tendency initially to overlook weak signals, then to overreact to emerging issues before we eventually take a more calibrated view. As you absorb the latest news, think critically about the source of the information before acting on it.

3) Don't assume that information creates informedness.

In our connected world, employees have direct access to many sources of information. Leaders might reasonably conclude that there is so much information and commentary available externally that they don't need to do anything additional. We have found, however, that creating and widely sharing a regularly updated summary of facts and implications is invaluable, so that time is not wasted debating what the facts are — or worse, making different assumptions about facts.

4) Use experts and forecasts carefully.

Experts in epidemiology, virology, public health, logistics, and other disciplines are indispensable in interpreting complex and shifting information. But it's clear that expert opinions differ on critical issues like optimal containment policies and economic impact, and it's good to consult multiple sources. Each epidemic is unpredictable and unique, and we are still learning about the critical features of the current one. We need to employ an iterative, empirical approach to understanding what's going on and what works — albeit one guided by expert opinion.

5) Constantly reframe your understanding of what's happening.

A big-picture synthesis of the situation and a plan to deal with it, once captured on paper, can itself become a source of inertia. A Chinese proverb reminds us that great generals should issue commands in the morning and change them in the evening.

But large organizations are rarely so flexible. Managers often resist disseminating plans until they are completely sure, and then they are reluctant to change them for fear of looking indecisive or misinformed, or of creating confusion in the organization. A living document, with a time-stamped "best current view" is essential to learn and adapt in a rapidly changing situation.

6) Beware of bureaucracy.

Controversial, sensitive, or high-profile issues will typically attract review by senior management, corporate affairs, legal, risk management, and a host of other functions. Each will have suggestions on how to best craft communications, leading to an overly generalized or conservative perspective and a slow, cumbersome process.

Assembling a small trusted team and giving them enough leeway to make rapid tactical decisions is critical. Overly managing communications can be damaging when each day brings significant new information to light. Use the clock speed of external events as a guideline for pacing the internal process, rather than starting with the latter as a given.

A living digital document can enhance speed by avoiding the rigamarole of issuing and approving multiple documents, and also reduces risk, since it can easily be updated or withdrawn as necessary. Furthermore, distinguishing clearly between facts, hypotheses, and speculations can help in communicating a fuller and more nuanced picture.

7) Make sure your response is balanced across these seven dimensions:

- *Communications:* Employees will likely be exposed to conflicting information and feel anxious or confused about the best course of action. Be sure to communicate policies promptly, clearly, and in a balanced manner. Furthermore, communicate contextual information and the reasoning behind policies so that employees can deepen their own understanding and also take initiative in unanticipated situations, such as employee holidays in a restricted location or how to handle contractors.
- *Employee needs:* Restrictions on travel and congregation will trigger employee needs for access to education, health care, daily provisions and the like. You should anticipate and develop solutions to these and create an information hub where employees can find all the information they need. Many of these needs will be locally specific, requiring a multi-tiered approach to policy making.
- *Travel:* Make sure that travel policies are clear in terms of where employees can travel to, for what reasons, what authorizations are required and when the policy will be reviewed.
- *Remote work:* Be clear on your policies — where they apply, how they will work, and when they will be reviewed. Home working is rare in some geographies, like China for example, and the need for additional explanation should be anticipated.

- *Supply-chain stabilization:* Attempt to stabilize supply chains by using safety stocks, alternative sources, and working with suppliers to solve bottlenecks. Where rapid solutions are not possible, co-develop plans, put in place interim solutions, and communicate plans to all relevant stakeholders.
- *Business tracking and forecasting:* It's likely that the crisis will create unpredictable fluctuations. Put in place rapid-reporting cycles so that you can understand how your business is being affected, where mitigation is required, and how quickly operations are recovering. A crisis doesn't imply immunity from performance management, and sooner or later markets will judge which companies managed the challenge most effectively.
- *Being part of the broader solution:* As a corporate citizen you should support others in your supply chain, industry, community, and local government. Consider how your business can contribute, be it in health care, communications, food, or some other domain. Focus on the intersection between acute social needs and your specific capabilities — in other words, live your purpose.

8) Use resilience principles in developing policies.

Efficiency reigns in a stable world with no surprises, and this mindset is often dominant in large corporations. But the key goal in managing dynamic and unpredictable challenges is *resilience* – the ability to survive and thrive through unpredictable, changing, and potentially unfavorable events. Our research on resilient systems shows that they generally have six common characteristics which should be reflected in crisis responses.

- *Redundancy*: Access to additional manufacturing capacity can help smooth supply-chain fluctuations. In the short term, companies may need to look beyond normal sources for solutions, but in the longer term, redundancy can be designed in.
- *Diversity*: Having multiple approaches to fulfillment can be less efficient but more flexible and resilient in crisis situations. Equally a diversity of ideas can greatly enhance solution development. Put together a cognitively diverse crisis management team that will have more ideas about potential solutions, especially if the corporate culture encourages expression of and respect for diverse perspectives. Beware of treating the crisis in one-dimensional manner — as a financial or logistical problem only, and staff your crisis team accordingly.
- *Modularity*: Highly integrated systems may be efficient, but they are vulnerable to avalanches of knock-on effects or even total system collapse if disturbed. In contrast, a modular system — where factories, organizational units or supply sources can be combined in different ways — offers greater resiliency. When a key brake valve supplier for Toyota was burned to the ground some years ago, supply was restored in just days because of the ability to swap production between suppliers, even of very different components. Ask how you can rewire your supply system in a modular manner both in the short and longer term.

- *Evolvability*: Systems can be built for optimization and peak efficiency or they can be built for evolvability — constant improvement in the light of new opportunities, problems, or information. Responses to dynamic crises like Covid-19 put a premium on evolvability. There is no knowable right answer, and any predetermined answer is likely to be wrong or to become obsolete over time. But it is possible to iterate and learn towards more effective solutions. While many lessons will be learned in retrospect, doing something now, seeing what works and remobilizing around the results is likely to be most effective strategy in the short term.

- *Prudence*: We cannot predict the course of events or their impacts for Covid-19, but we can envision plausible downside scenarios and test resilience under these circumstances. We can run scenarios for a widespread global epidemic, a multi-regional epidemic, and a rapidly contained epidemic, for example. Now that the focus has shifted from containment of the Covid-19 epidemic in China to preventing its establishment in new epicenters overseas, we have arrived at another inflection point, with very high uncertainty. It would be prudent for companies to take a fresh look at worst-case scenarios and develop contingency strategies against each.

- *Embeddedness*: Companies are stakeholders in wider industrial, economic, and social systems which are also under great stress. Those who fail to look at their supply chains or ecosystems holistically will have limited impact. Solutions that solve for an individual company at the expense of or neglecting the interests of others will create mistrust and damage the business in the longer term. Conversely, support to customers, partners, health care, and social systems in a time of adversity can potentially create lasting goodwill and trust. A key element of dealing with economic stress is to live one's values precisely when we are most likely to forget them.

9) Prepare now for the next crisis.

Covid-19 is not a one-off challenge. We should expect additional phases to the current epidemic and additional epidemics in the future. Our research on the effectiveness of organizational responses to dynamic crises indicates that there is one variable which is most predictive of eventual success – preparation and preemption. Preparing for the next crisis (or the next phase of the current crisis) now is likely to be much more effective than an ad hoc, reactive response when the crisis actually hits.

10) Intellectual preparation is not enough.

Many companies run scenarios to create intellectual preparedness for unexpected situations. Scenarios must be updated and customized, however, in the light of the most material risks to a business at any given time. Those risks have shifted even over the last few days, with the rise of new disease epicenters.

Intellectual preparedness alone is not enough, however. Something can be well understood but unrehearsed as a capability. Scenarios should therefore ideally be backed up by war gaming to simulate and learn from behaviors under stress. A war room set-up, with a small dedicated team empowered to decide and execute, can cut through organizational complexity.

11) Reflect on what you've learned.

Rather than heaving a sigh of relief and returning to normal routines when the crisis subsides, efforts should be made not to squander a valuable learning opportunity. Even while the crisis is unfolding, responses and impacts should be documented to be later reviewed and lessons distilled. Rapidly evolving situations expose existing organizational weaknesses, like an inability to make hard decisions or an excessive bias towards consensus, which constitute opportunities for improvement.

For example, airline safety is one of the most effective global learning systems we have in this respect. Each time there is an incident from minor mishaps to tragic accidents resulting in lives lost, root causes are investigated in forensic detail according to pre-agreed protocols, and binding recommendations are made. It's not surprising that flying has become one of safest forms of travel, thanks to cumulative learnings and adaptations from previous misfortunes.

12) Prepare for a changed world.

We should expect that the Covid-19 crisis will change our businesses and society in important ways. It is likely to fuel areas like online shopping, online education, and public health investments, for example. It is also likely to change how companies configure their supply chains and reinforce the trend away from dependence on few mega-factories. When the urgent part of the crisis has been navigated, companies should consider what this crisis changes and what they've learned so they can reflect them in their plans.

Martin Reeves is a senior partner and managing director in the San Francisco office of BCG and chairman of the BCG Henderson Institute, BCG's think tank on management and strategy. He can be reached at reeves.martin@bcg.com.

Nikolaus Lang is a senior partner and managing director in BCG Germany and global leader of the Global Advantage Practice. He can be reached at Lang.Nikolaus@bcg.com.

Philipp Carlsson-Szlezak is a partner and managing director in BCG's New York office and chief economist of BCG. He can be reached at: Carlsson-Szlezak.Philipp@bcg.com.

Harvard Business Review

HEALTH

8 Questions Employers Should Ask About Coronavirus

by Jeff Levin-Scherz and Deana Allen

MARCH 02, 2020 UPDATED **MARCH 15, 2020**

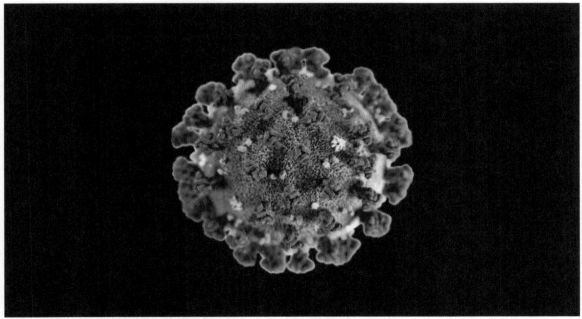

THE CENTERS FOR DISEASE CONTROL AND PREVENTION

The coronavirus outbreak that originated in Wuhan, China has spread to at least 144 countries and has sickened more than 204,000 people, with more than 8,000 deaths (click here for the latest data). Governments have shut borders and imposed quarantines, and companies have imposed travel bans. The human and economic impacts on businesses have been stark.

This epidemic is a wake-up call for companies to carefully review the strategies, policies, and procedures they have in place to protect employees, customers, and operations in this and future epidemics. Here are eight questions that companies should ask as they prepare for — and respond to — the spread of the virus.

1. How can we best protect our employees from exposure in the workplace?

The coronavirus that causes Covid-19 (as the disease is called) is thought to spread largely through respiratory droplets from coughing and sneezing, and it seems to spread easily. It may also be possible to become infected by touching a contaminated surface or object and then touching one's nose or mouth. The Centers for Disease Control and Prevention advises that employees should:

- Stay home if they have respiratory symptoms (coughing, sneezing, shortness of breath) and/or a temperature above 100.4 F.
- Leave work if they develop these symptoms while at the workplace.
- Shield coughs and sneezes with a tissue, elbow, or shoulder (not the bare hands).
- Wash hands often with soap and water for at least 20 seconds or use an alcohol-based hand sanitizer.

We would add that it's sensible to avoid shaking hands entirely to reduce the risk of spreading infection. Though that might be awkward at times, it's an increasingly common practice in hospitals and clinics.

As hand washing is one of the most effective defenses, employers need to make sure that employees have ready access to washing facilities and that those are kept well stocked with soap and (ideally) paper towels; there is some evidence that paper towel drying is less likely to spread viruses than jet dryers. Alcohol-based hand sanitizers and sanitizing wipes should be distributed throughout the workplace, and all frequently touched surfaces such as workstations, countertops and doorknobs should be routinely cleaned. Increased cleaning of common areas using standard cleaning agents can also reduce risk of spread of respiratory disease. Unless they're delivering health care, there's no need for organizations to stockpile face masks, as these are in short supply and the CDC doesn't recommend their use by healthy people to protect against infection.

(For more on employers' role, see the CDC's "Interim Guidance for Businesses and Employers" here.)

A just-completed Willis Towers Watson survey of 158 employers globally, over half of them multinational companies, found that most are implementing an array of actions to protect employees. As might be expected, China is out ahead on this. Nearly 90% of surveyed companies there have increased employee access to hand sanitizers, and more than 80% have ramped up public health communications (such as posters about preventing spread) and are directing employees to work from home if they can. In North America where Covid-19 is just starting to emerge, companies are being proactive: 70% have already or plan to increase communications, and more than half have or plan to increase access to hand sanitizers.

2. When should we exclude workers or visitors from the workspace?

As discussed, employees should stay home or go home if they have symptoms of coronavirus infection. But dedicated staff often resist taking sick days, instead dragging themselves into work where they may infect others. Given the threat this epidemic presents, managers shouldn't hesitate to send employees who present with Covid-19 symptoms home. Likewise, employees or visitors who are symptomatic or at high risk for Covid-19 should be kept separate from staff and helped with arrangements to leave the workplace and obtain medical evaluation while minimizing their public exposure. For example, they should avoid public places and public transportation, and, ideally, should stay six feet away from others unless they are wearing a mask.

If Covid-19 becomes widespread in the community, companies can check temperatures using hand-held thermal scanners and consider excluding staff or visitors with temperatures over 100.4 F. Temperature is not an exceptionally accurate way to assess risk, though, as some with the coronavirus will be contagious but have no fever, and others will have higher temperatures not related to this virus. Thus, an elevated temperature in combination with respiratory symptoms is the best indicator of possible infection.

Public health organizations recommend that companies bar employees or visitors from coming to the workplace for a period 14 days after a "medium" or "high-risk" exposure to the virus — generally meaning having been in close contact with someone who is known to be infected, or having traveled from a high-risk region. (For more, see the CDC's "Guidance for Risk Assessment.") Forty-three percent of North American employers in our survey said they now bar employees or visitors who have recently traveled from China for a period of 14 days after return. Visits or return to the workplace can resume after 14 days if no symptoms emerge.

3. Should we revise our benefits policies in cases where employees are barred from the worksite or we close it?

The likelihood that increasing numbers of employees will be unable to work either because they are sick or must care for others means that companies should review their paid time off and sick leave policies now. Policies that give employees confidence that they will not be penalized and can afford to take sick leave are an important tool in encouraging self-reporting and reducing potential exposure. Our employer survey found that nearly 40% of employers have or plan to clarify their pay policy if worksites are closed or employees are furloughed.

While few companies outside of Asia have closed worksites yet because of the epidemic, about half of the Chinese companies we surveyed had shut down worksites at least temporarily. Such closures will likely become more common outside of Asia should the epidemic continue on its current course.

Most firms will treat Covid-19 in their policies as they would any other illness, and sick leave or short-term disability insurance would be applicable. However, exclusion from the workplace might not be covered by disability policies, and prolonged absence could last longer than available sick leave. Our survey found that more than 90% of employers in China paid their workers in full and maintained full benefits during furloughs. Companies should promulgate clear policies on this now and communicate about these with employees. Most will want to offer protections to their workforce to the extent this is financially feasible.

4. Have we maximized employees' ability to work remotely?

While many jobs (retail, manufacturing, health care) require people to be physically present, work, including meetings, that can be done remotely should be encouraged if coming to work or traveling risks exposure to the virus. Videoconferencing, for instance, is a good alternative to risky face-to-face meetings. Nearly 60% of the employers we surveyed indicated that they have increased employees' flexibility for remote work (46%) or plan to (13%).

5. Do we have reliable systems for real-time public health communication with employees?

Dangerous rumors and worker fears can spread as quickly as a virus. It is imperative for companies to be able to reach all workers, including those not at the worksite, with regular, internally coordinated, factual updates about infection control, symptoms, and company policy regarding remote work and circumstances in which employees might be excluded from or allowed to return to the workplace. These communications should come from or be vetted by the emergency response team, and they should be carefully coordinated to avoid inconsistent policies being communicated by different managers or functions. Clearly this requires organizations to maintain current phone/text and email contact information for all employees and test organization-wide communication periodically. If you don't have a current, universal contact capability already, now is a good time to create this.

6. Should we revise our policies around international and domestic business travel?

Sixty-five percent of companies surveyed are now restricting travel to and from Asia. It is prudent to limit employee business travel from areas where Covid-19 is most prevalent — both to prevent illness and to prevent loss of productivity due to quarantine or employee exclusion from the workplace after travel. Companies should track the CDC Travel Health Notices and the State Department Travel Advisories to determine what business travel should be canceled or postponed. The CDC currently recommends that travelers avoid all nonessential travel to China, South Korea, Europe and Iran.

Employees should be especially careful not to travel if they feel unwell, as they might face quarantine on return if they have a fever even without significant risk of coronavirus infection.

7. Should we postpone or cancel scheduled conferences or meetings?

Yes. There is mounting evidence that social distancing can delay the epidemic and potentially save lives, so most meetings and conferences should be converted from in-person to virtual. Some states and localities are banning meetings of more than 250 people. If you have a meeting, limit the number of attendees and encourage those who are older or have chronic disease to attend virtually. Provide room to allow attendees to sit or stand at least six feet away from others. Discourage hand-shaking and assure that proper handwashing facilities (and/or hand sanitizers) are easily available. If you have any questions about best practices, contact your local health department.

8. Are supervisors adequately trained?

Sixty-five percent of companies surveyed that have employees in China are training supervisors about implications of Covid-19, while 34% of those with employees in North America report they are actively training or planning to train their supervisors. Whatever form the training takes, supervisors should have ready access to appropriate information (such as on infection control and company policies) and should know who to contact within the firm to report exposures. Supervisors or other designated persons in the company should promptly notify local public health authorities about any suspected exposure. A web search for "local health department" and postal code or city or county name will generally yield accurate contact information. In the US, supervisors can also contact the CDC at 800-232-4636 with questions about coronavirus.

Diligent planning for global health emergencies can help protect employees, customers, and the business. But plans are only as good as their execution. Companies should use the current situation to optimize and battle-test their plans. Effective employer action in the face of the COVID-19 pandemic can save lives and help companies earn the long-term trust of their employees and customers.

Editor's Note: This article was updated on March 18, 2020 to include the latest data and public health recommendations.

Jeff Levin-Scherz, MD, MBA, is a senior director and co-leader of the North American Health Management practice at Willis Towers Watson. Jeff trained as primary care physician, and has played leadership roles in provider organizations and a health plan. He is an Assistant Professor at the Harvard TH Chan School of Public Health.

Deana Allen RN, MBA, is a senior vice president of the North America Healthcare Industry practice and serves as the Intellectual Capital and Operations Excellence leader at Willis Towers Watson. In addition to work as a clinician she has served as a health system corporate director of risk and insurance and healthcare consultant.

Harvard
Business
Review

OPERATIONS MANAGEMENT

Prepare Your Supply Chain for Coronavirus

by James B. Rice, Jr.
FEBRUARY 27, 2020

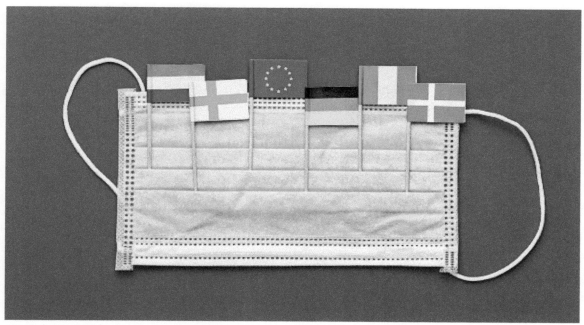

KIRA-YAN/GETTY IMAGES

Developing a cogent supply chain response to the coronavirus outbreak is extremely challenging, given the scale of the crisis and the rate at which it is evolving.

The best response, of course, is to be ready before such a crisis hits, since options become more limited when a disruption is in full swing. However, there are measures that can be taken now even if you're not fully prepared. And although its long-term consequences have yet to fully play out, the coronavirus outbreak already provides some lessons about how you can better prepare your company to deal with future large-scale crises.

What You Can Do Now

Let's first look at some actions that can be taken to mitigate the impacts of the crisis on supply chains.

Start with your people. The welfare of employees is paramount, and obviously people are a critical resource. The companies that recovered the fastest after Hurricane Katrina in 2005 were those that tracked down all their employees who dispersed across the southeastern United States. Procter & Gamble even went so far as to create a local employee village on high ground with housing, foodstuffs, and cash advances for employees and their families.

It may be necessary to rethink work practices. When an ice storm shut down Louisville, Kentucky, in 2009, local workers could not get to UPS's sorting hub. But workers could still travel by air, so the company flew in personnel from other cities to keep the hub running. This interchangeability depended on job and equipment standardization.

Maintain a healthy skepticism. Accurate information is a rare commodity in the early stages of emerging disasters, especially when governments are incentivized to keep the population and business community calm to avoid panic. Impact reports tend to be somewhat rose-tinted. However, local people can be a valuable and more reliable source of information, so try to maintain local contacts.

Run outage scenarios to assess the possibility of unforeseen impacts. Expect the unexpected, especially when core suppliers are in the front line of disruptions. In the case of the coronavirus crisis, China's influence is so wide-ranging that there will almost inevitably be unexpected consequences. Inventory levels are not high enough to cover short-term material outages, so expect cause widespread runs on common core components and materials.

In 2005, Hurricane Rita struck Houston and western Louisiana, causing widespread shutdowns of oil refining assets located in the region. What came as a surprise to consumer-packaged-goods firms some six months later was that petroleum-based packaging was in short supply because of Rita's impact on supplies of the raw materials needed to make these materials. Many firms scrambled to redesign packaging using old-style paper and cardboard.

Create a comprehensive, emergency operations center. Most organizations today have some semblance of an emergency operations center (EOC), but in our studies we've observed that these EOCs tend to exist only at the corporate or business unit level. That's not good enough — a deeper, more detailed EOC structure and process is necessary. EOCs should exist at the plant level, with predetermined action plans for communication and coordination, designated roles for functional representatives, protocols for communications and decision making, and emergency action plans that involve customers and suppliers.

Designing for response

The coronavirus story will undoubtedly add to our knowledge about dealing with large-scale supply chain disruptions. Even at this relatively early stage, we can draw important lessons about managing crises of this nature that should be applied down the road.

Know all your suppliers. Map your upstream suppliers several tiers back. Companies that fail to do this are less able to respond or estimate likely impacts when a crisis erupts. After the 2011 Sendai earthquake in Japan, it took weeks for many companies to understand their exposure to the disaster because they were unfamiliar with upstream suppliers. At that point any available capacity was gone. Similarly, develop relationships in advance with key resources — it's too late after the disruption has erupted.

Understand your critical vulnerabilities and take action to spread the risk. Many supply chains have dependencies that put firms at risk. An example is when an enterprise is dependent on a supplier that has a single facility with a large share of the global market. The Sendai disaster highlighted this type of exposure. For example, Hitachi manufactured approximately 60% of the global supply of airflow sensors, a critical component for auto manufacturers. The anticipated shortage of these items forced some automotive original-equipment manufacturers (OEMs) to ration the remaining airflow sensors to their highest margin product lines. The coronavirus outbreak has exposed Apple's and many auto OEMs' dependency on sourcing from China.

Create business continuity plans. These plans should pinpoint contingencies in critical areas and include backup plans for transportation, communications, supply, and cash flow. Involve your suppliers and customers in developing these plans.

Don't forget your people. A backup plan is needed for people too. The plan may include contingencies for more automation, remote-working arrangements, or other flexible human resourcing in response to personnel constraints.

Revisit Your Supply Chain's Design

Until very recently, most global companies could base their supply chain designs on the assumption that materials flow freely globally, enabling them to source, produce, and distribute products at the lowest-cost locations around the world. U.S.-China trade policy whiplash, Brexit, and now the coronavirus crisis have challenged the validity of this fundamental assumption. Specifically, the coronavirus illustrates the vulnerability of having so many sources located in one spot — and a spot that is far away from critical markets in North America, Europe, and Latin America.

We believe that a new kind of design is needed that enables companies to rapidly reconfigure their supply chains and be ultra-agile and responsive to rapidly changing global trade policies, supply dynamics, and disruptions. Therefore, the question is: How should companies design their supply chains to operate effectively in a highly volatile world where consumers are intolerant of tardy responses? There are many options, and each one involves tradeoffs between the level of risk that the enterprises can tolerate and the amount of operational flexibility it wants to achieve. Here are two examples:

Redesign with second sources. This supply-chain design provides backup capacity for supply, production, and distribution outages. The backup capacity spreads the risk of a disruption across two sources (as long as the disruption does not also affect the second source location). Consequently, it is better to have a second source outside the primary source region. Although this supply chain design lowers risk levels, it incurs higher administrative, quality monitoring, and unit costs. Also, economies of scale vary according to the amount of supply allocated to each supply source.

Redesign to source locally. This design calls for a company to have production facilities with local sources of supply in each of its major markets. Like the above option, it spreads the risk. Since these sources are dispersed, the economies of scale are lower and the capital costs are higher, but the transportation costs are lower.

These are gross simplifications of many design options that the firm can take to reduce risk and ensure response capacity. A more detailed analysis and assessment is necessary. Obviously, in selecting a design, companies have to weigh the costs of each and how it will affect their ability to serve their customers and compete against other firms. Deciding which design is optimal is not a one-time process. Firms should regularly revisit and challenge their design choices and the strategies that underpin them.

It's impossible to anticipate the arrival of global crises such as the coronavirus outbreak, but firms can mitigate their impacts by taking supply chain preparedness to a higher level. They should act before a disruption occurs and adjust and execute new plans afterward rather than starting from scratch every time they are plunged into a new crisis.

James B. Rice, Jr. is deputy director of the MIT Center for Transportation & Logistics.

Harvard Business Review

PERSONNEL POLICIES

What Are Companies' Legal Obligations Around Coronavirus?

by Peter Susser and Tahl Tyson

MARCH 04, 2020

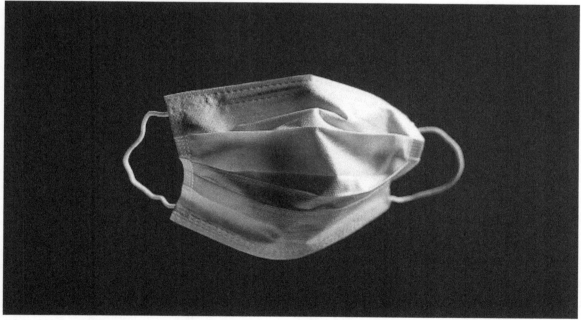

ALEKSANDR ZUBKOV/GETTY IMAGES

With the rapid global spread of coronavirus, companies should focus first and foremost on employee safety. And as they're reviewing their strategies, policies, and procedures, many leaders are specifically wondering about their legal risk. Not having adequate communicable-illness policies and response plans could expose them to a laundry list of HR-related legal concerns.

Most countries have laws designed to protect employees from physical harm at work. In the United States, employees are protected under the Occupational Safety and Health Act, so if an employee becomes infected at work, in some circumstances the employer may face penalties. Unprepared employers may be exposed to lawsuits related to workers' compensation, invasion of privacy, discrimination, unfair labor practice, and negligence.

The good news is that with careful attention to employee safety and legal preparedness, employers can minimize employees' risk of infection and their own legal risks. Following are eight steps companies should take to these ends. The value of these efforts, of course, is relevant to any life-threatening infectious disease, not just coronavirus.

Stay informed

Start by identifying authoritative sources of public health guidance on the epidemic, and stay up to date on officially recommended and mandated actions in the applicable jurisdictions. These sources include The Centers for Disease Control and Prevention, The World Health Organization, The European Center for Disease Prevention and Control, and country-specific public health guidance such as this for Singapore and this for the United Kingdom.

This official guidance should serve as the foundation for organizational decisions about health- and legal-risk mitigation. Being able to demonstrate corporate policy alignment with official recommendations can be an important legal safeguard in cases where the company's infection-control efforts are challenged.

Intensify communications and hygiene

For legal and practical reasons, companies need to be able to show that they have given employees accurate information about ways to prevent the spread of infection — and that they have provided people with the means to act on that information. Thus, organizations should educate employees, in advance of any workplace infection, about modes of transmission and symptoms by sharing specific public health guidelines and, more broadly, directing staff to the official sources of information on which the organization will rely.

In addition, employers must implement measures to reduce the risk of workplace transmission. For example, public health guidance for reducing transmission includes ensuring that employees have easy access to handwashing facilities and/or hand sanitizers and that public surfaces such as counters, doorknobs, and elevator buttons are regularly disinfected. Employers may also consider changes to reduce overcrowding, such as facilitating remote work, shift work, and perhaps physical layout changes. Such measures may help protect workers from infection and help protect organizations from liability.

Employers should also instruct staff to inform management if they have been exposed to the virus or show symptoms of infection, or if they, or a member of their household, have particular vulnerabilities such as a weakened immune system that may require enhanced protections from infection. Further, staff with symptoms of infection should be sent home or instructed to stay home, and visitors who have been exposed or who have symptoms should be excluded from the workplace. Failure to provide this guidance can potentially expose a company to liability should employees become infected in the workplace and it can be shown that management had not communicated about this policy. (Although disability discrimination laws protect employees with covered health conditions, limitations can generally be imposed if there's a direct threat to the health or safety of others.)

Consider restrictions on returning to work

While employers risk discrimination claims if they base decisions to restrict employees from work on grounds of race or national origin, they can impose reasonable, fact-based restrictions if there is a direct threat to the health or safety of others. An employer can judge, by applying official guidelines or with input from a medical consultant, whether and when an employee who has been ill or who has potentially been exposed can safely return to work. Written policies should be explicit about when employees with potentially transmissible conditions will and will not be allowed back, and relevant communications should be documented.

Be mindful of an employer's duty of care

Most countries have laws designed to protect employees from physical harm at work. For multinational employers and those with mobile employees, it is important to identify the applicable country laws (which may be more than those of a single jurisdiction in some cases), as one size will not fit all.

In the United States, employees are protected under the Occupational Safety and Health Act (OSH Act). Section 5(a)(1) of the OSH Act is the general duty clause, which requires employers to provide their employees with a workplace "free from recognized hazards ... likely to cause death or serious physical harm." The federal Occupational Safety and Health Administration (OSHA) can cite employers for violating the general duty clause if there is a recognized hazard and they do not take reasonable steps to prevent or abate the hazard. However, OSHA citations can only be based on standards, regulations, or the general duty clause.

State-mandated workers' compensation programs, and a separate program for federal workers, provide benefits to eligible employees who suffer job-related injuries and illnesses (these vary state by state). As a rule, where the harm arises out of and in the course of employment, employees are limited to the prescribed workers' compensation benefits and cannot recover damages for pain and suffering or mental anguish. Some states allow additional awards — beyond normal workers' compensation awards — when injury results from an employer's "willful" or "intentional" act, which might include failure to provide appropriate protections.

Businesses also have to consider liability to third parties, such as customers, which may not be so limited. For example, a restaurant employee infected on the job will only be entitled to workers' compensation, but theoretically the patrons they may infect could seek greater damages.

Evaluate leave and pay

Employers should analyze their legal obligations to provide employees with leave in the event of sickness or disability and evaluate whether their policies need to be adjusted in the current circumstances. In the U.S., the Family and Medical Leave Act (FMLA), the Americans with Disabilities Act (ADA), and state workers' compensation laws will apply, as well as any contract and policy language. Exclusions from insurance policies should be identified — for example, many travel insurance policies exclude pandemics.

Drawing on this analysis, companies should consider under which circumstances they would want to extend or expand benefits and protections, and they should evaluate their level of income protection for employees on leave, perhaps adjusting benefits plans for employees who exceed their sick-day allotment in order to support sick employees who must stay home.

It is important to look beyond the immediate legal requirements to the broader business and legal implications. For example, a business may not be legally required to pay an employee during a period it bars him or her from the workplace because that individual was on personal travel to a place where transmission was occurring. However, choosing not to do so makes it more likely that they prematurely return to work, thereby infecting other staff, risking business continuity, legal liability from third parties such as customers, and contributing to an increase in infections.

Alleviate stress and anxiety

Stress and anxiety related to coronavirus infection could also become a legal concern. The legal standards will vary by jurisdiction. For example, employers in the United Kingdom have a duty to assess the risk of stress-related, ill health arising from work activities, and they are required to take reasonable measures to control such risks. In some cases, this may mean taking steps beyond the minimum if doing so is not unduly burdensome to the employer and mitigates the psychological burden on the employee. For example, rather than terminating the employee for refusing to come to the office due to fear of contagion, even though all officially recommended precautions have been taken, an employer might be more flexible in allowing time off or remote working arrangements. Such steps can help U.K. employers avoid claims of unfair dismissal.

Employers should be aware that mental health conditions such as germophobia may be protected as a disability under laws such as the Americans with Disabilities Act and require that employers take a modified approach pursuant to reasonable accommodation requirements.

Protect privacy

Employers should understand which personal health data an employee might be obligated to disclose if he or she becomes infected or is at high risk for infection — likely, anything that could interfere with the employee's ability to perform the essential functions of the job, or that could increase the risk to coworkers or third parties through workplace contact. Failure to understand the legal obligations in relation to such data could expose the company to breach of privacy claims.

Fortunately, even rigorous privacy rules allow employers to disclose employees' protected health information to authorities for public health purposes. That said, all such data must be handled within the organization's data privacy protection framework, and if such data is being transmitted from the European Union to the United States, care should be taken to do so in compliance with the General Data Protection Regulation (GDPR).

Plan for a worst-case scenario

Contingency planning may include, for example, temporary succession planning for key decision-makers, and understanding and preparing in advance for the legal requirements in cases of furloughs and layoffs. Many jurisdictions require more formal procedures and notifications for layoffs above a certain number of employees. A failure to comply can have severe penalties for employers and even personal liability in some cases for their leadership. Planning ahead in order to stay compliant is an important part of an organization's resilience program.

Peter Susser (psusser@littler.com) is partner in the global employment and labor law firm, Littler Mendelson, based in Washington, D.C.

Tahl Tyson (ttyson@littler.com) is a partner in the global employment and labor law firm, Littler Mendelson. She is a U.K. solicitor based in Seattle, Washington.

Harvard Business Review

RECESSION

The Coronavirus Crisis Doesn't Have to Lead to Layoffs

by Atta Tarki, Paul Levy and Jeff Weiss

MARCH 20, 2020

SANCHIT KHANNA/HINDUSTAN TIMES/GETTY IMAGES

During a crisis, the path between corporate denial and layoffs is often a short one. For weeks, our corporate clients and contacts waved off concerns about a potential economic impact from the Covid-19 outbreak. Then something changed around March 9. First, our contacts told us they were restricting visitors to their offices and encouraging remote work. Now, only a few days later, we are hearing that many them are considering layoffs to ensure they make it through the crisis — and a recent survey found that a vast majority of corporate leaders are considering some sort of financial action as a result of the pandemic.

To be sure, a cost-cutting reflex is understandable. Leaders are obligated to make responsible decisions to keep their companies afloat. But those who manage the economic effects of this crisis in a clear and compassionate way create more value for their companies and will come out of this pandemic stronger than ever before. So before announcing deep layoffs, we recommend that you consider these measures first.

Communicate Openly

Many leaders assume that if they admit that the company is facing turbulent times it will scare away its best employees. The assumption is that these employees will worry less if management holds their cards close to their chest. Nothing could be further from the truth. Everyone knows that we are going through a global pandemic. Everyone knows certain sectors of the economy are already getting hit hard by changes in consumer behavior as a result of this virus. And everyone knows a slowdown in parts of the economy and increased uncertainty might impact their company as well.

Instead of forcing your employees to second-guess what might be in store for them, be utterly clear with them about the financial health of your firm and what goals you will prioritize. These goals will not be the same for every company, and you shouldn't communicate empty statements you don't believe in, such as "we put our employees first." These statements can be confusing and even counterproductive when people are worried about their jobs. It's better for you to be specific. For example, if your goal is to save jobs while meeting your bank covenants, say that. If it is to make a series of changes swiftly to shore up job security, clarify that you are prioritizing that decision over other, slower changes.

Share the Pain

If you are doing cut backs to save job losses, you must lead by example and do cut backs that impacts your own day-to-day as well. If you don't, there is a danger that your staff will feel like saps, doing sacrifices while the C-suite continues unaffected. Get a commitment for a pay cut from your senior leaders. As CEO, you should take the largest salary cut yourself. Several airline CEOs, for example, are temporarily forgoing salaries or taking pay cuts amid looming cutbacks for the industry.

Consider Crowdsourcing Ideas with Employees

It can be overwhelming to open the floor for ideas from employees on what the company should do. You might fear that employees will be resentful if their ideas are not selected. You might also fear that asking your employees for ideas means that you will appear to have less control. We know one CEO who slapped down the idea of such open consultation, saying, "Participation is one thing, pandemonium is another." But crowdsourcing doesn't have to be equivalent to chaos. In our experience, it is critical that you ask your employees to voice their ideas. By showing them, not just saying, that you care about what they think, you will have stronger buy-in for the initiatives you eventually prioritize.

For example, when Beth Israel Deaconess Medical Center (BIDMC) undertook a crowd-sourcing approach to cost-cutting following the 2008 financial crisis, most of the comments were positive; indeed, employees appreciated the openness so much that they defended the moves to disgruntled colleagues who wanted to lash out or sabotage the process.

To begin the crowdsourcing process, leaders should offer structure by articulating that you intend to prioritize initiatives with lower capital requirements, lower risk profiles, proven positive impact on cash flow, higher chances of saving jobs, and so on. Then truly demonstrate that you are open to the ideas of the staff. You might even present the final packages to the staff and let them indicate their preferences between the various options. The bottom line is, you lose no control by this kind of approach. You enhance your standing as a leader.

Review All the Options (Even the Less Conventional Ones)

Before layoffs, consider all your non-obvious options for reducing cost. A four-day work week for roles where you have excess capacity will reduce staff cost by nearly 20% (assuming some costs will remain due to overhead and benefits). Some employees might agree to working half-time if they know that doing so will save jobs.

You can also offer employees the opportunity for unpaid leave if they so wish — framing this leave as a "sabbatical" can help take some of the stigma of the absence away. In fact, you might find that some employees welcome these options and wish they could have had them all along. By making it clear that one of your overriding goals is to avoid layoffs, you might find that employees are amenable to the personal sacrifices inherent in salary-increase freezes, halting bonuses, bans on overtime, pausing of payments into retirement funds, reduction of vacation days, and other cost-saving measures.

Consider decelerating pay decreases for lower salary ranges to protect employees who are the most vulnerable. For example, you might reduce salaries of your highest paid employees by 10%, mid-range salaried employees by 5%, and everyone else above a certain threshold by half of that. This is what was done at BIDMC during its cost-reduction—and employees appreciated that senior leaders tried all sorts of creative approaches to minimize head-count reduction.

Have "Ice in the Belly"

Being a leader in turbulent times can be nerve wracking. If you act too fast, it might turn out that you overreacted. If you act too slow, the business might go under. It would be wise to have what in

Swedish is called *Is i magen*, "ice in the belly," roughly translated as your ability to keep your cool in a critical situation.

First, recognize that as bad as things look, government assistance may be forthcoming. Many business leaders recall that there was resistance toward economic stimulus packages in the aftermath of the 2008 financial crisis. Part of that resistance was due to public resentment towards bailing out financial institutions that had caused the crisis. The public is more likely to be supportive of economic stimulus packages in the current case where the downturn is hard to blame on one particular industry. And economic aid might also be targeted towards companies that can prevent layoffs.

Furthermore, don't treat all negative indicators for your business the same. If your client is a movie theater and they need to pause your project, you have reason to believe they will not be able to pick the project back up anytime soon since the theater industry is taking a big financial hit. However, if your client is a hospital that says they'd like to pause your project so that they can focus on the high volume of patients at the moment, it's worthwhile showing their management team that you understand their current priorities.

It's also reasonable to explain to them that you are trying to understand what the economic impacts of this pandemic will be on your firm and ask them if they can have an open discussion with you to help you understand how likely it is that they will continue the project once things calm down.

But *Is i magen* does not mean that you are cool to the needs of your staff. This is a time to show empathy, rather than maintaining an emotional distance from your people. Lead with compassion, especially for the most vulnerable members of your company. One common misconception is that most people primarily look out for themselves in turbulent times. On the contrary, our experience is that during a crisis, individuals overwhelmingly prefer to make sacrifices if it means that their company can help more of their colleagues keep their jobs.

Going through a downturn and making tough decisions to keep your company afloat is hard. However, if you lead with compassion you will touch the lives of your employees in an extraordinary way and come out of this potential slowdown stronger than ever before, enhancing the shared values of your staff.

Atta Tarki is the founder and CEO of specialized executive-search and project-based staffing firm ECA. He is also the author of the book, *Evidence Based Recruiting* (McGraw Hill, February 2020). Find him on Twitter: @AttaTarki

Paul Levy was CEO of Beth Israel Deaconess Medical Center in Boston from 2002 to 2011. His actions to avoid layoffs during the Global Financial Crisis led to worldwide attention and acclaim for his hospital. He is the author of *Goal Play! Leadership Lessons from the Soccer Field*. Find him on Twitter: @Paulflevy

Jeff Weiss is founder and managing director of CCI, a national CEO network, and Assistant professor, adjunct at UCLA School of Medicine.

Harvard
Business
Review

TECHNOLOGY

Delivery Technology Is Keeping Chinese Cities Afloat Through Coronavirus

by Chengyi Lin
MARCH 17, 2020

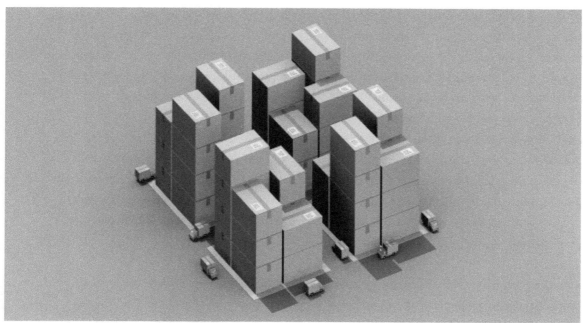

JORG GREUEL/GETTY IMAGES

For the last month, China's cities, with their empty streets and deserted shopping malls, have looked like the set of a post-apocalypse TV series. It may be a glimpse of the future for Europe and North America, where lockdowns are quickly expanding.

Public discourse in Europe and the U.S. is predictably focused on how bad things will get and the practicalities of life under lockdown: How will people get food supplies? Can the medical services cope? Will people get paid?

But even at this stage in the lifecycle of the Covid-19 pandemic, some lessons are already emerging from China about how we can cope with the social and commercial disruption of this kind. A key driver, it turns out, is digital technology.

Let's start by looking at China, where the most recent signs suggest that the epidemic has now stabilized. In Wuhan — a city of 11 million people — the lockdown posed a serious problem. Because it was the first city affected, its citizens were unprepared for what they faced. Initially, the lockdown imposed by the Chinese authorities triggered panic buying of food and other essential items, emptying supermarket shelves.

Yet in a matter of days, supplies began to flow into Wuhan. Although fears and concerns about the disease ran high, residents fairly quickly came to terms with the lockdown and have leveraged digital technology to organize and collaborate with suppliers, thereby ensuring that supplies have reached the people who need them the most. Two factors have contributed to this remarkable show of resilience:

- **Digitally Enabled Delivery Systems:** In China's major cities, groceries and other items purchased online can be delivered to the home within as little as 20 minutes following a purchase. This is largely down to the deployment of digital technology. Alibaba's Cainiao network, for example, supports the supply chains of the merchants it serves via an AI-enabled digital inventory system that links the online and offline shopping worlds, in which merchants' physical stores serve an extended distribution network. As a result, almost as soon as the lockdown was declared in Wuhan, Alibaba was shipping medical and food supplies into the province.
- **Consumer Comfort with the Online World:** In the past five years, Alibaba Group, JD.com, MTDP (Meituan Dianping) and many other companies have transformed the purchasing behavior of Chinese consumers, moving them away from bricks-and-mortar shopping into online spaces, often consolidated through a so-called "super app." As of 2019, China's e-commerce penetration had, by one estimate, reached 36.6% of retail sales, with 71% of Chinese consumers transacting online at some point, mostly via smartphone apps (80% of e-commerce transactions).

The combination of consumer digital maturity and digitally supported supply chains has enabled local residents to organize home delivery of essential supplies to people in self-quarantine. In the gated communities and neighborhoods that characterize Beijing, for example, residents have organized small groups of volunteers via group chat apps to receive supplies at the gate for the whole community, box them for each household, and deliver them to people's doorsteps.

In the U.S. and Europe, however, the digital landscape seems rather less favorable for this kind of response than in China.

Although U.S. consumers are more than ready to shop on Amazon and other e-commerce platforms, only 16% of total sales in 2019 were on e-commerce platforms — a number achieved in China four years earlier.

Moreover, groceries and ready-to-eat food remain challenging categories in the digital world, despite efforts to experiment with home delivery of foodstuffs on the part of Walmart.com and Amazon, which recently purchased Whole Foods. U.S. consumers have been much slower to shift to the digital marketplace in these categories than the Chinese, while last-mile logistics for the grocery category have yet to reach the standards seen in China's major cities. Even in the restaurant business, the likes of Uber Eats and others lag far behind China's MTDP, Ele.me, and many other similar services in China.

Europe, unfortunately, is even further behind. Although large retailers such as Ooshop.com of Carrefour and start-ups like Deliveroo are building last-mile logistical capacities, consumer demand and readiness are low, while old city infrastructures and labor regulations make the rapid construction of an efficient delivery system an extremely challenging proposition.

Just last fall, while Alibaba and Amazon celebrated their achievements during the Singles' Day and Thanksgiving sales respectively, large merchants in Europe ran into serious difficulties in handling their logistics for "Black Friday" sales. I personally received apologetic letters and cancelation messages from a major French electronic retailer, which admitted, "We had unforeseeable difficulties in handling the large amount of transactions during the Black Friday period." That is forgivable if all that happened was that one failed to impress a friend with a new gadget. When feeding their children is the issue, consumers will be less indulgent.

Of course, the pandemic will subside – and Americans and Europeans will find ways to cope with its effects; the Chinese do not have a monopoly on creativity and solidarity. But as the U.S. and Europe emerge from the coronavirus epidemic, their governments, cities, and businesses should look at how China's digital advantages have helped it respond to the logistic challenges presented by the crisis. Covid 19 is a wakeup call for European and the U.S., which both need to accelerate the digital transformation of their economies — ahead of the next pandemic.

Chengyi Lin is an affiliate professor in strategy at INSEAD in Fontainebleau, France

Harvard Business Review

ECONOMICS & SOCIETY

How Chinese Companies Have Responded to Coronavirus

by Martin Reeves, Lars Fæste, Cinthia Chen, Philipp Carlsson-Szlezak and Kevin Whitaker

MARCH 10, 2020

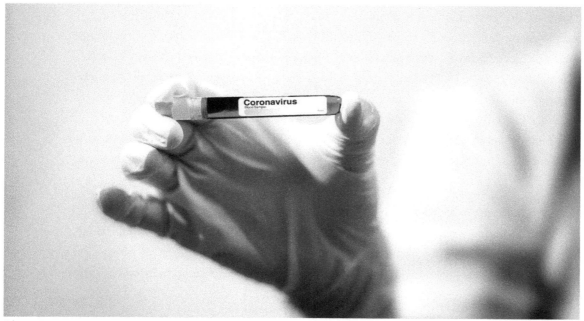

THIRAWATANA PHAISALRATANA/EYEEM/GETTY IMAGES

As the Covid-19 crisis spreads to new epicenters in Europe and the U.S., companies are scrambling to mobilize responses. There are no easy answers, due to the unpredictability of disease dynamics, a lack of relevant prior experience, and the absence of plug-and-play instructions from government or international authorities.

Clearly each local situation is different, but we believe there are opportunities for companies to learn from others in regions that are weeks ahead in responding to the epidemic. China appears to be in the early stages of an economic rebound, according to our analysis of high-frequency data on proxies for the movement of people and goods, production, and confidence. While this recovery could be vulnerable if a new wave of local infections were to emerge, many Chinese companies have already moved beyond crisis response to recovery and post-recovery planning.

Based on our experience supporting Chinese enterprises with their recovery plans, we have extracted 12 early lessons for leaders elsewhere. To be sure, China has its own distinct political and administrative systems, as well as social customs, but many of the lessons here seem broadly applicable.

1. Look ahead and constantly reframe your efforts.

By definition, crises have a highly dynamic trajectory, which requires a constant reframing of mental models and plans. Initial ignorance gives way to discovery and sense-making, then crisis planning and response, recovery strategy, post-recovery strategy, and finally, reflection and learning. This process must be fast — and therefore CEO-led — to avoid getting stuck in complex internal coordination processes and being slow to react to changing circumstances.

In China, some of the fastest-recovering companies proactively looked ahead and anticipated such shifts. For example, in the early stages of the outbreak, Master Kong, a leading instant noodle and beverage producer, reviewed dynamics on a daily basis and reprioritized efforts regularly. It anticipated hoarding and stock-outs, and it tilted its focus away from offline, large retail channels to O2O (online-to-offline), e-commerce, and smaller stores. By continuously tracking retail outlets' re-opening plans it was also able to adapt its supply chain in a highly flexible manner. As a result, its supply chain had recovered by more than 50% just a few weeks after the outbreak, and it was able to supply 60% of the stores that were reopened during this period — three times as many as some competitors.

2. Use an adaptive, bottom-up approach to complement top-down efforts.

Rapid, coordinated responses require top-down leadership. But adapting to unpredictable change, with distinct dynamics in different communities, also requires decentralized initiative-taking. Some Chinese companies effectively balanced the two approaches, setting a top-down framework within which employees innovated.

For example, Huazhu, which operates 6,000 hotels in 400 cities across China, set up a crisis task force that met daily to review procedures and issued top-down guidance for the whole chain. In addition, it leveraged its internal information platform, an app called Huatong, to make sure employees and franchisees were armed with timely information. This allowed franchisees to adapt central guidance to their own local situations, in terms of disease conditions and local public health measures.

3. Proactively create clarity and security for employees.

In a crisis, it's hard to find clarity, when the situation and the available information are constantly changing, driven by the exponential logic of contagion. Official advice may be absent, contradictory, out of date, or not granular enough for practical purposes. Furthermore, confusion is compounded by a plethora of media reports with differing perspectives and advice. Employees will need to adopt new ways of working, but they won't be able to do so unless they have clear, consistent information and overall direction.

Some Chinese companies created very proactive guidance and support for employees. For example, China's largest kitchenware manufacturer Supor instituted very specific operational guidelines and procedures for its employees, such as instructions for limiting exposure while dining in canteens and emergency plans for abnormal situations. In addition, the company instituted health checks for employees and their families from the early stages of the outbreak and procured preventative equipment. It was well prepared for a timely resumption of work, reopening some production lines in the second week of February.

4. Reallocate labor flexibly to different activities.

In hard-hit businesses, such as restaurants, employees were unable to carry on their regular activities. Rather than furloughs or layoffs, some creative Chinese enterprises actively reallocated employees to new and valuable activities, like recovery planning, or even loaned them to other companies.

For example, in response to a severe decline in revenue, more than 40 restaurants, hotels, and cinema chains optimized their staffing to free up a large share of their workforces. They then shared those employees with Hema, a "new retail" supermarket chain owned by Alibaba, which was in urgent need of labor for delivery services due to the sudden increase in online purchases. O2O players, including Ele, Meituan, and JD's 7Fresh followed this lead by also borrowing labor from restaurants.

5. Shift your sales channel mix.

Person-to-person and bricks-and-mortar retail were severely restricted in affected regions. Agile Chinese enterprises rapidly redeployed sales efforts to new channels both in B2C and B2B enterprises.

For example, cosmetics company Lin Qingxuan was forced to close 40% of its stores during the crisis, including all of its locations in Wuhan. However, the company redeployed its 100+ beauty advisors from those stores to become online influencers who leveraged digital tools, such as WeChat, to engage customers virtually and drive online sales. As a result, its sales in Wuhan achieved 200%growth compared to the prior year's sales.

6. Use social media to coordinate employees and partners.

With remote working and a new set of complex coordination challenges, many Chinese companies took to social media platforms, such as WeChat, to coordinate employees and partners.

Impact of Covid-19 in China: Emerging Signs of Recovery

China appears to be in the early stage of an economic rebound, according to data for three benchmarks.

People and goods are starting to move again.

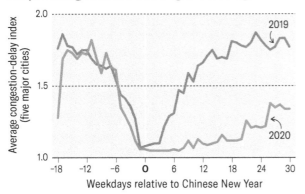

Coal consumption is increasing, which indicates that production is resuming.

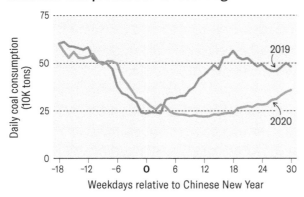

Property transactions are resuming, signaling that confidence isn't broken.

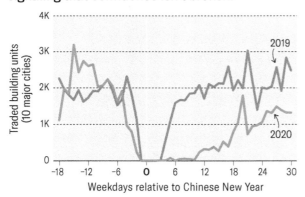

Note: Data re-based for weekdays excluding weekends relative to start of Chinese New Year (Feb. 5, 2019, and Jan. 25, 2020). Cities in the congestion-delay index are Beijing, Shanghai, Guangzhou, Shenzhen, and Wuhan. Daily coal consumption is the sum of averages from Jerdin Electric, Guangdong Yudean Group, Datang International Power Generation, and Huaneng Power International. Cities analyzed for building units traded are Beijing, Shanghai, Guangzhou, Shenzhen, Hangzhou, Nanjing, Qingdao, Suzhou, Nanchang, and Xiamen.
Source: Wind, cqcoal.com, and BCG Center for Macroeconomics ▽ HBR

For example, Cosmo Lady, the largest underwear and lingerie company in China, initiated a program aimed at increasing its sales through WeChat, enlisting employees to promote to their social circles. The company created a sales ranking among all employees (including both the chairman and CEO), helping motivate the rest of the staff to participate in the initiative.

7. Prepare for a faster recovery than you expect.

Only six weeks after the initial outbreak, China appears to be in the early stages of recovery. Congestion delays currently stand at 73% of 2019 levels, up from 62% at the worst part of the epidemic, indicating that the movement of people and goods is resuming. Similarly, coal consumption appears to be recovering from a trough of 43% to currently 75% of 2019 levels, indicating that some production is resuming. And confidence appears to be coming back as seen in real estate transactions, which had fallen to 1% of 2019 levels but have since bounced back to 47%.

While the depth and duration of the economic impact in other countries is impossible to forecast, China's experience points to a scenario that companies should prepare for. Considering the time it takes to formulate, disseminate, and apply new policies in large companies, recovery planning needs to start while you're still reacting to the crisis.

For example, a premium Chinese travel agency, facing a collapse in its short-term business, refocused around longer-term preparations. Instead of reducing headcount, it encouraged employees to use their time to upgrade internal systems, improve skills, and design new products and services to be better prepared for the eventual recovery.

8. Expect different recovery speeds for different sectors.

Unsurprisingly, sectors and product groups recover at different speeds, thus requiring distinct approaches. Stock prices fell across all sectors in the first two weeks that China's epidemic accelerated, but leading sectors, such as software and services, and healthcare equipment and services, recovered within a few days and have since increased by an average of 12%. The bulk of sectors recovered more slowly but reached prior levels within a few weeks. And the hardest-hit sectors — such as transportation, retail and energy, representing 28% of market capitalization for China's largest stocks — are still down by at least 5% and showing only minimal signs of recovery.

This means companies need to calibrate their approach by business — and large companies need to calibrate their approach by division. For example, a large global food & beverage conglomerate used the crisis to accelerate the long-term shifts in its product mix in China (the company's second largest market worldwide), including increasing its focus on health-relevant products, imported products, and on online sales channels.

9. Look for opportunity amid adversity.

While the crisis in China impacted all sectors to some extent, at a more granular level, demand increased in many specific areas. These include B2C e-commerce (especially door-to-door models), B2B e-commerce, remote meeting services, social media, hygiene products, health insurance, and other product groups. Some Chinese players mobilized rapidly to address these needs.

For example, Kuaishou, a social video platform valued at $28 billion, promoted online education offerings to compensate for school and university closures. The company and other video platforms partnered with the Ministry of Education to open a national online cloud classroom to serve students. And a major restaurant chain leveraged down-time to plan a new offering of semi-finished dishes, capturing the increased need and occasion for home cooking during the crisis.

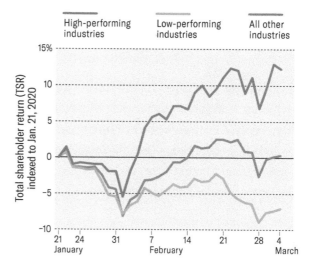

Covid-19 Recovery Dynamics Differ Across Sectors in China

Note: Based on the 500 largest companies by market cap in Greater China as of Jan. 1, 2020; industry groups based on GICS classifications; industry groups with indexed TSR >5% as of March 4, 2020, are classified as high performers; TSR <-5% classified as low performers
Source: S&P Capital IQ, BCG Henderson Institute Analysis ⨀ **HBR**

10. Adapt your recovery strategy by location.

Regional public health policies, disease dynamics, and administrative guidance will create recovery dynamics that vary by location — likely not following the geographical structure of companies. This requires a flexible approach.

For example, a leading Chinese dairy company (a $10bn business with a wide production base and deep national distribution in China) developed a segmented approach based on regional and city recovery dynamics, as well as on its own supply chain infrastructure, and salesforce density. The planned supply from factories in severely impacted areas was allocated to factories in other regions in a phased approach. Marketing activities, messaging, and budget allocation were also adjusted continually to reflect regional differences in expected recovery speed, consumer sentiment and needs.

11. Rapidly innovate around new needs.

Beyond rebalancing your product portfolio, new customer needs also create opportunities for innovation. When threatened by crisis, many companies will be focused on defensive moves, but some Chinese companies boldly innovated around emerging opportunities.

The insurance industry is notoriously conservative, but in response to the crisis, Ant Financial added free coronavirus-related coverage to its products. The action served a customer need, while promoting awareness of the company's online offerings and improving customer loyalty. It expects a 30% increase in health insurance income in February, as compared to the previous month.

12. Spot new consumption habits being formed.

Some shifts will likely persist beyond the crisis, and many sectors will reemerge to new market realities in China and elsewhere. Indeed, the SARS crisis is often credited with accelerating the adoption of e-commerce in China. It is too early to say for sure which new habits will stick in the long run, but some strong possibilities include a leap from offline to online education, a transformation in health care delivery, and an increase in B2B digital channels.

Some Chinese companies are already planning around these shifts in the post-crisis world. For example, the Chinese business of a global confectionary manufacturer accelerated its existing digital transformation efforts. The company canceled offline campaigns for Valentine's Day and other promotional activities, reinvesting resources instead into digital marketing, WeChat programs, and partnerships with O2O platforms to take advantage of new consumer behaviors during the outbreak and beyond.

***

Undoubtedly more new lessons will emerge from China, Korea, Italy, and eventually the U.S. Companies that adopt a high-frequency approach to learning, codifying and applying lessons from other regions will be better able to protect their employees and business. Indeed, in a fast changing, volatile world, such an adaptive approach should be applied more broadly beyond crisis management.

Martin Reeves is a senior partner and managing director in the San Francisco office of BCG and chairman of the BCG Henderson Institute, BCG's think tank on management and strategy. He can be reached at reeves.martin@bcg.com.

Lars Fæste is a managing director and senior partner in BCG's Hong Kong office and leader of BCG's Greater China system. He can be reached at faeste.lars@bcg.com.

Cinthia Chen is a managing director and partner in BCG's Hong Kong office, and China head of BCG's Center for Customer Insight. She can be contacted at chen.cinthia@bcg.com.

Philipp Carlsson-Szlezak is a partner and managing director in BCG's New York office and chief economist of BCG. He can be reached at: Carlsson-Szlezak.Philipp@bcg.com.

Kevin Whitaker is the head of strategic analytics at BCG Henderson Institute. He can be reached at whitaker.kevin@bcg.com.

SECTION 2
MANAGING REMOTE TEAMS

Harvard Business Review

LEADING TEAMS

15 Questions About Remote Work, Answered

by Tsedal Neeley

MARCH 16, 2020

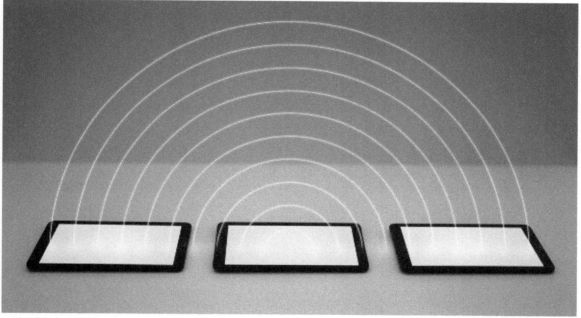

JORG GREUEL/GETTY IMAGES

The coronavirus pandemic is expected to fundamentally change the way many organizations operate for the foreseeable future. As governments and businesses around the world tell those with symptoms to self-quarantine and everyone else to practice social distancing, remote work is our new reality. How do corporate leaders, managers, and individual workers make this sudden shift? Tsedal Neeley, a professor at Harvard Business School, has spent two decades helping companies learn how to manage dispersed teams. In this edited Q&A, drawn from a recent HBR subscriber video call in which listeners were able to ask questions, she offers guidance on how to work productively at home, manage virtual meetings, and lead teams through this time of crisis.

Are organizations prepared for this sudden transition?

The scale and scope of what we're seeing, with organizations of 5,000 or 10,000 employees, asking people to work from home very quickly, is unprecedented. So, no, organizations are not set up for this.

What's the first thing that leaders and individual managers can do to help their employees get ready?

Get the infrastructure right. Do people have the requisite technology or access to it? Who has a laptop? Will those who do [have laptops] be able to dial into their organizations easily? Will they have the software they need to be able to do work, have conference calls, etc? What about the employees who don't have laptops or mobile devices? How do you make sure that they have access to the resources they need to do work? Direct managers have to very quickly ensure that every employee has full access, so no one feels left behind.

What should people who aren't accustomed to remote work do to get psychologically ready for it?

Develop rituals and have a disciplined way of managing the day. Schedule a start and an end time. Have a rhythm. Take a shower, get dressed, even if it's not what you'd usually wear to work, then get started on the day's activities. If you're used to moving physically, make sure you build that into your day. If you're an extrovert and accustomed to a lot of contact and collaboration with others, make sure that still happens. Ask yourself: How will I protect myself from feeling lonely or isolated and stay healthy, productive, and vibrant? Create that for yourself.

Remember that you might actually enjoy working from home. You can play the music you like. You can think flexibly about your time. It can be fun. As for managers, they need to check in on people. Make sure not only that they're set up but also that they have a rhythm to their day and contact with others. Ask: "What can I do to make sure that this sudden and quick transition is working for you?"

How should those check-ins happen? As a group? In one-on-ones? Via phone calls? Or video chats?

First, you should have a group conversation about the new state of affairs. Say, "Hey, folks, it's a different world. We don't know how long this is going to last. But I want to make sure you all feel that you have what you need." This should be followed by a team launch to jump-start this new way of working. Figure out: How often should we communicate? Should it be video, phone, or Slack/Jive/ Yammer. If you're not using one of those social media systems, should you? What's the best way for us to work together? You've got to help people understand how to do remote work and give them confidence that it will work.

Once those things are sorted out, meet with your group at least once a week. In a remote environment, frequency of contact cannot go down. If you're used to having meetings, continue to do so. In fact, contact should probably go up for the whole team and its members. Newer employees, those working on critical projects, and people who need more contact will require extra one-on-ones. Remember, too, that you can do fun things virtually: happy hour, coffee breaks, lunch together. All these things can help maintain the connections you had at the office. There's ample research showing that virtual teams can be completely equal to co-located ones in terms of trust and collaboration. It just requires discipline.

How does working from home affect psychological health? What can employers do to make sure that people are staying focused, committed, and happy?

People lose the unplanned watercooler or cappuccino conversations with colleagues in remote work. These are actually big and important parts of the workday that have a direct impact on performance. How do we create those virtually? For some groups and individuals, it will be constant instant messaging. For others, it will be live phone conversations or video conferences. Some people might want to use WhatsApp, WeChat, or Viber. A manager can encourage those types of contact points for psychological health. People are not going to be able to figure these things out organically. You've got to coach them. One more piece of advice: Exercise. It's critical for mental well-being.

What are the top three things that leaders can do to create a good remote culture?

There are more than 10,000 books in the English language on Amazon on virtuality and how to lead remotely or at a distance. Why is that? Because this is very difficult to do, and managers have to actively work on it. Number one, make sure that team members constantly feel like they know what's going on. You need to communicate what's happening at the organizational level because when they're at home, they feel like they've been extracted away from the mothership. They wonder what's happening at the company, with clients, and with common objectives. The communication around those are extremely important. So you're emailing more, sharing more.

During this period, people will also start to get nervous about revenue goals and other deliverables. You'll have to make sure they feel like they're going to be OK. Another thing is to ensure that no members feel like they have less access to you than others. At home, people's imaginations begin to go wild. So you have to be accessible and available to everyone equally. Finally, when you run your group meetings, aim for inclusion and balance the airtime so everyone feels seen and heard.

How will these changes affect productivity?

Productivity does not have to go down at all. It can be maintained, even enhanced, because commutes and office distractions are gone. Of course, you might be at home with your partner or kids and those issues will need to be worked out. Another problem might be your ability to resolve problems quickly when you can't meet in person, in real time. That might create delays. But other than that, I don't see productivity going down. There's robust evidence showing that it shouldn't change.

If the social distancing **policies go on for a while, how do you measure your employees' productivity and eventually review them on that work?**

I'll say this to every manager out there: you have to trust your employees. This is an era and a time in which we have to heed Ernest Hemingway's advice: "The best way to find out if you can trust somebody is to trust them." You can't see what people are doing. But equip them in the right ways, give them the tasks, check on them like you've always done, and hope they produce in the ways you want them to. You can't monitor the process, so your review will have to be outcome-based. But there's no reason to believe that, in this new environment, people won't do the work that they've been assigned. Remote work has been around for a very long time. And today we have all of the technologies we need to not only do work but also collaborate. We have enterprise-wide social media tools that allow us to store and capture data, to have one-to-many conversations, to share best practices, and to learn.

Let's talk about virtual meetings. **What are some best practices, beyond the general advice to clarify your purpose, circulate an agenda, prepare people to be called on, and so forth?**

First, you have to have some explicit ground rules. Say, "Folks, when we have these meetings, we do it in a nice way, we turn off of phones, we don't check emails or multitask." I highly recommend video conferencing if you have the ability to do that. When people are able to see one another, it really makes a difference. And then you trust people to follow the ground rules.

Number two, because you no longer have watercooler conversations, and people might be just learning how to work from home, spend the first six to seven minutes of a meeting checking in. Don't go straight to your agenda items. Instead, go around and ask everyone, "How are you guys doing?" Start with whomever is the newest or lowest status person or the one who usually speaks the least. You should share as well, so that you're modeling the behavior. After that, you introduce the key things you want to talk about and again model what you want to see, whether it's connecting, asking questions, or even just using your preferred technology, like Zoom or Skype for Business.

The last thing is you have to follow up these virtual meetings with redundant communication to ensure that people have heard you and that they're OK with the outcome. Say you have a video conference about a topic. You follow it up with an email or a Slack message. You should have multiple touchpoints through various media to continue the trail of conversation.

And how do you facilitate highly complex or emotionally charged conversations when people aren't face to face?

You can only raise one or two of these topics because you don't have the time or opportunity to work things through after the meeting. You can't just walk to people's offices to follow up. So, be very thoughtful about what you bring up and when and how you do it. But you can still have these conversations. Allowing people to disagree in order to sharpen the team's thinking is a very positive thing. Sometimes, in virtual environments, people don't feel psychologically safe, so they might not speak up when they should. And so you might even want to generate or model a little of disagreement — always over work, tasks or processes, of course, never anything personal.

In light of various daycare and school closings, how do you discuss children and childcare?

Leaders should be prepared for that conversation and to help people think those issues through. The blurring of boundaries between work and home has suddenly come upon us, so managers have got to develop the skills and policies to support their teams. This might involve being more flexible about the hours in which employees work. You don't have to eat lunch at 12pm. You might walk your dog at 2pm. Things are much more fluid, and managers just have to trust that employees will do their best to get their work done.

We've talked about internal communication, but what advice do you have for people in client-facing functions?

We've been seeing virtual sales calls and client engagements. You do the exact same things. Here, it's even more important to use visual media. Take whatever you would be doing face-to-face and keep doing it. Maybe you can't wine and dine. But you can do a lot. Be creative.

What do you do in an organization where you have a mix of both blue- and white-collar workers? Or for those colleagues who aren't properly equipped?

The organizations have to figure out a way to support those workers: some kind of collective action to help them because otherwise you're completely isolating people who are critically important to your operation. I would put together a task force, and I would find solutions to keep them connected and ensure that they still feel valued. And include them in the planning.

If you sense that, despite your best efforts, an employee is struggling, not focused, lonely, what can you do?

When you see the signs — like fewer emails or more inhibition in group conversations — talk to them. Increase contact and encourage others to, as well. Understand where they are. And get them what they need. Organizations should also make sure to have employee assistance services at this time. When you're suddenly taking away people's regular routines and connection with others, and it's open ended, some will struggle and need extra help. I would add that every CEO of every organization needs to be much more visible right now — through video conferencing or taped recordings to give people confidence, calm them down, and be healers- or hope-givers-in-chief.

Do you see this crisis changing the way all teams and organizations operate going forward?

I think it's going to broaden their repertoires. Organizations, teams, and people will experiment more with virtual work. Many of them have always wanted to test it as way of expanding their reach or labor force. It's not that people are going to permanently adopt this new format of work, but this experience will expand everyone's capacity. If there's a tiny positive aspect to this mess we're finding ourselves in, it's that we're developing certain skills that could helpful in the future. That's my deepest hope.

Tsedal Neeley is the Naylor Fitzhugh Professor of Business Administration in the Organizational Behavior Unit at Harvard Business School and the founder of the consulting firm Global Matters. She is the author of *The Language of Global Success*. **Twitter:** @tsedal

Harvard Business Review

LEADING TEAMS

A Guide to Managing Your (Newly) Remote Workers

by Barbara Z. Larson, Susan R. Vroman and Erin E. Makarius

MARCH 18, 2020

In response to the uncertainties presented by Covid-19, many companies and universities have asked their employees to work remotely. While close to a quarter of the U.S. workforce already works from home at least part of the time, the new policies leave many employees — and their managers — working out of the office and separated from each other for the first time.

Although it is always preferable to establish clear remote-work policies and training in advance, in times of crisis or other rapidly changing circumstances, this level of preparation may not be feasible. Fortunately, there are specific, research-based steps that managers can take without great effort to improve the engagement and productivity of remote employees, even when there is little time to prepare.

Common Challenges of Remote Work

To start, managers need to understand factors that can make remote work especially demanding. Otherwise high-performing employees may experience declines in job performance and engagement when they begin working remotely, especially in the absence of preparation and training. Challenges inherent in remote work include:

Lack of face-to-face supervision: Both managers and their employees often express concerns about the lack of face-to-face interaction. Supervisors worry that employees will not work as hard or as efficiently (though research indicates otherwise, at least for some types of jobs). Many employees, on the other hand, struggle with reduced access to managerial support and communication. In some cases, employees feel that remote managers are out of touch with their needs, and thereby are neither supportive nor helpful in getting their work done.

Lack of access to information: Newly remote workers are often surprised by the added time and effort needed to locate information from coworkers. Even getting answers to what seem like simple questions can feel like a large obstacle to a worker based at home.

This phenomenon extends beyond task-related work to interpersonal challenges that can emerge among remote coworkers. Research has found that a lack of "mutual knowledge" among remote workers translates to a lower willingness to give coworkers the benefit of the doubt in difficult situations. For example, if you know that your officemate is having a rough day, you will view a brusque email from them as a natural product of their stress. However, if you receive this email from a remote coworker, with no understanding of their current circumstances, you are more likely to take offense, or at a minimum to think poorly of your coworker's professionalism.

Social isolation: Loneliness is one of the most common complaints about remote work, with employees missing the informal social interaction of an office setting. It is thought that extraverts may suffer from isolation more in the short run, particularly if they do not have opportunities to connect with others in their remote-work environment. However, over a longer period of time, isolation can cause any employee to feel less "belonging" to their organization, and can even result in increased intention to leave the company.

Distractions at home: We often see photos representing remote work which portray a parent holding a child and typing on a laptop, often sitting on a sofa or living-room floor. In fact, this is a terrible representation of effective virtual work. Typically, we encourage employers to ensure that their remote workers have both dedicated workspace and adequate childcare before allowing them to work remotely. Yet, in the case of a sudden transition to virtual work, there is a much greater chance that employees will be contending with suboptimal workspaces and (in the case of school and daycare closures) unexpected parenting responsibilities. Even in normal circumstances family and home demands can impinge on remote work; managers should expect these distractions to be greater during this unplanned work-from-home transition.

How Managers Can Support Remote Employees

As much as remote work can be fraught with challenges, there are also relatively quick and inexpensive things that managers can do to ease the transition. Actions that you can take today include:

Establish structured daily check-ins: Many successful remote managers establish a daily call with their remote employees. This could take the form of a series of one-on-one calls, if your employees work more independently from each other, or a team call, if their work is highly collaborative. The important feature is that the calls are regular and predictable, and that they are a forum in which employees know that they can consult with you, and that their concerns and questions will be heard.

Provide several different communication technology options: Email alone is insufficient. Remote workers benefit from having a "richer" technology, such as video conferencing, that gives participants many of the visual cues that they would have if they were face-to-face. Video conferencing has many advantages, especially for smaller groups: Visual cues allow for increased "mutual knowledge" about coworkers and also help reduce the sense of isolation among teams. Video is also particularly useful for complex or sensitive conversations, as it feels more personal than written or audio-only communication.

There are other circumstances when quick collaboration is more important than visual detail. For these situations, provide mobile-enabled individual messaging functionality (like Slack, Zoom, Microsoft Teams, etc.) which can be used for simpler, less formal conversations, as well as time-sensitive communication.

If your company doesn't have technology tools already in place, there are inexpensive ways to obtain simple versions of these tools for your team, as a short-term fix. Consult with your organization's IT department to ensure there is an appropriate level of data security before using any of these tools.

And then establish "rules of engagement": Remote work becomes more efficient and satisfying when managers set expectations for the frequency, means, and ideal timing of communication for their teams. For example, "We use videoconferencing for daily check-in meetings, but we use IM when something is urgent." Also, if you can, let your employees know the best way and time to reach you during the workday (e.g., "I tend to be more available late in the day for ad hoc phone or video conversations, but if there's an emergency earlier in the day, send me a text.") Finally, keep an eye on communication among team members (to the extent appropriate), to ensure that they are sharing information as needed.

We recommend that managers establish these "rules of engagement" with employees as soon as possible, ideally during the first online check-in meeting. While some choices about specific expectations may be better than others, the most important factor is that all employees share the same set of expectations for communication.

Provide opportunities for remote social interaction: One of the most essential steps a manager can take is to structure ways for employees to interact socially (that is, have informal conversations about non-work topics) while working remotely. This is true for all remote workers, but particularly so for workers who have been abruptly transitioned out of the office.

The easiest way to establish some basic social interaction is to leave some time at the beginning of team calls just for non-work items (e.g., "We're going to spend the first few minutes just catching up with each other. How was your weekend?"). Other options include virtual pizza parties (in which pizza is delivered to all team members at the time of a videoconference), or virtual office parties (in which party "care packages" can be sent in advance to be opened and enjoyed simultaneously). While these types of events may sound artificial or forced, experienced managers of remote workers (and the workers themselves) report that virtual events help reduce feelings of isolation, promoting a sense of belonging.

Offer encouragement and emotional support: Especially in the context of an abrupt shift to remote work, it is important for managers to acknowledge stress, listen to employees' anxieties and concerns, and empathize with their struggles. If a newly remote employee is clearly struggling but not communicating stress or anxiety, ask them how they're doing. Even a general question such as "How is this remote work situation working out for you so far?" can elicit important information that you might not otherwise hear. Once you ask the question, be sure to listen carefully to the response, and briefly restate it back to the employee, to ensure that you understood correctly. Let the employee's stress or concerns (rather than your own) be the focus of this conversation.

Research on emotional intelligence and emotional contagion tells us that employees look to their managers for cues about how to react to sudden changes or crisis situations. If a manager communicates stress and helplessness, this will have what Daniel Goleman calls a "trickle-down" effect on employees. Effective leaders take a two-pronged approach, both acknowledging the stress and anxiety that employees may be feeling in difficult circumstances, but also providing affirmation of their confidence in their teams, using phrases such as "we've got this," or "this is tough, but I know we can handle it," or "let's look for ways to use our strengths during this time." With this support, employees are more likely to take up the challenge with a sense of purpose and focus.

We'll add our own note of encouragement to managers facing remote work for the first time: you've got this. Let us know in the comments your own tips for managing your remote employees.

Barbara Z. Larson is executive professor of management and director of partnerships at Northeastern's D'Amore-McKim School of Business. Her research focuses on the personal and interpersonal skills that people need to work effectively in virtual environments, and she works with collaborators in both academia and industry to develop training methods and materials to enable more productive virtual work. Prior to her academic career, Professor Larson worked for 15 years in international finance and operations leadership, most recently as Director of International Finance at R.R. Donnelley.

Susan R. Vroman is a lecturer of management at Bentley University. Her research interests include the impact leadership enactment has on organizational culture and employee engagement, with specific focus on supporting flexible work arrangements. Prior to her academic career, Dr. Vroman worked for over 20 years as an organizational effectiveness and strategic human resource management executive and advisor. She continues this work in a consulting capacity.

Erin E. Makarius an associate professor of human resources in the management department of the College of Business Administration at the University of Akron and received her Ph.D. from The Ohio State University. Dr. Makarius has several years of experience in human resources and management, including working at and consulting with a variety of companies in the financial, insurance, and consumer products industries. Her research interests include boundary spanning in the form of technological, international, and organizational boundaries, with emphasis on the role of relationships and reputation in these processes.

Harvard Business Review

What It Takes to Run a Great Virtual Meeting

by Bob Frisch and Cary Greene

MARCH 05, 2020

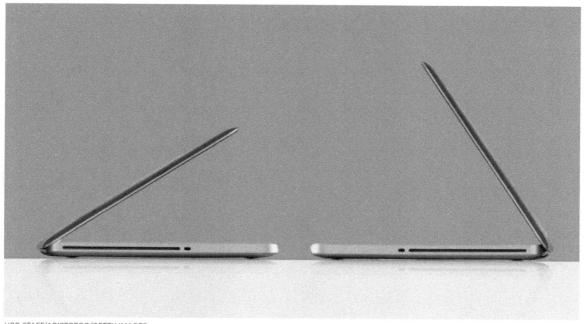

HBR STAFF/ARISTOTOO/GETTY IMAGES

As companies scramble to protect employees from the spreading coronavirus with travel restrictions and remote work arrangements, there's a distinct possibility that in-person meetings with teams, customers, or suppliers may be canceled for days — or potentially weeks.

Under the best of circumstances, as soon as one or two attendees "dial in" to any meeting, productivity starts to suffer. There's a long list of reasons. Attendees often interpret virtual meetings as a license to multi-task. Meeting organizers tend to be less careful with the purpose and design of the conversation. And it's not uncommon for one or two attendees to dominate the discussion while others sit back and "tune out."

But it doesn't have to be this way. Virtual meetings — even impromptu one's sparked by fears of a contagion — can be run more effectively, using basic meeting best practices and easy-to-use, inexpensive technology.

Here are 12 steps you can take to make that happen:

1. Use video. To make people feel like they're all at the "same" meeting, use video conferencing rather than traditional conference dial-ins. Technology — such as Zoom, Skype, and GoToMeeting — helps to personalize the conversation and to keep participants engaged.

2. That said, always provide an audio dial-in option. Video conferencing can work very well, but it relies on a strong internet connection that may not always be available. People need the ability to participate via audio, but make it clear that video-first is the new norm.

3. Test the technology ahead of time. Nothing kills momentum at the start of a meeting like a 15-minute delay because people need to download software, can't get the video to work, etc. Prior to a virtual meeting, all participants should test the technology and make sure they are comfortable with the major features. And remember, supplier or customer conversations may require your team to familiarize themselves with different software packages.

4. Make sure faces are visible. Video conferences are more effective when people can see each other's facial expressions and body language. Ask individuals to sit close to their webcam to help to recreate the intimacy of an in-person meeting.

5. Stick to meeting basics. Prior to the conversation, set clear objectives, and send a pre-read if appropriate. During the session, use an agenda, set meeting ground rules, take breaks, and clearly outline next steps (including timing and accountabilities) after each section and at the end of the meeting.

6. Minimize presentation length. The only thing worse than a long presentation in person is a long presentation during a virtual meeting. Meetings should be discussions. Background information should be provided beforehand. If someone needs to present, use screen sharing to guide the conversation, so attendees can literally "be on the same page." But prioritize conversation to maximize the time people are looking at each other.

7. Use an icebreaker. Although we're not big fans of them, it's important to use every tool to reinforce interpersonal relationships when people may be feeling isolated. Also, it's important to know if a participant may have a close friend or relative fighting the virus, so some type of "check in" is in order.

8. Assign a facilitator. It's usually harder to manage a virtual discussion than an in-person one. It can be helpful to assign one individual to guide the conversation, allowing the other participants to focus on the content. The facilitator can also use a polling system to "take the pulse" of the group on certain questions and ensure that all voices are heard. The facilitator should also be able to resolve basic questions on the technology being used.

9. Call on people. Getting everyone to participate without talking over each other is one of the more challenging aspects of running a virtual meeting. To forestall this, we recommend periodically calling on individuals to speak, even by virtually "going around the table" before a decision is finalized. Some software packages even allow attendees to "raise a hand" if they want to. This can help the facilitator drive closure without the risk of excluding an introverted participant's views.

10. Capture real-time feedback. Gathering and processing high-quality input during a virtual meeting can be challenging, especially since visual cues are harder to read. Use a phone-based survey tool like Poll Everywhere to collect on-demand feedback from attendees on specific topics in real time. Keep the polling open, separate from the videoconference to avoid disrupting the conversation. Participants will need clear instructions on how to use the system and practices, but groups get the hang of it very quickly and it's well worth the effort.

11. Don't be afraid to tackle tough issues. Meeting virtually is a learned behavior, and you'll be amazed how much you can get out of it once you and your team begin to be comfortable working this way. It may seem natural to wait to discuss tough issues until everyone is in person, but that may not be an option. So don't shy away from controversial topics.

12. Practice once or twice while you're still together. Hold your next staff meeting virtually, with each executive sitting in their office and hooking into the meeting with no assistance. After the meeting concludes, gather and debrief about the experience. What went well, and what didn't? How can you evolve your virtual meetings to make them as productive as when you meet in person?

Not being able to work together in the same room with colleagues may become a major challenge in the next few weeks. To make virtual meetings work, you might need to adjust how your team conducts them. But a small investment in preparedness now could have a huge impact if that time comes.

Bob Frisch is the managing partner of the Strategic Offsites Group, a Boston-based consultancy. He is also the co-author of *Simple Sabotage* (HarperOne, 2015), the author of *Who's In The Room?* (Jossey-Bass, 2012), and four *Harvard Business Review* articles, including "Off-Sites That Work" (June 2006).

Cary Greene is a partner of the Strategic Offsites Group, a Boston-based consultancy, and co-author of *Simple Sabotage* (HarperOne, 2015) and the *Harvard Business Review* article "Leadership Summits that Work" (March 2015). He writes frequently for HBR.org.

SECTION 3
LEADING THROUGH THE CRISIS

Harvard
Business
Review

MEETINGS

How to Get People to Actually Participate in Virtual Meetings

by Justin Hale and Joseph Grenny

MARCH 09, 2020

SORAPOP/GETTY IMAGES

These days it's hard to get people to pay attention in any meeting, but when people aren't in the same room, it can be especially difficult. And it's particularly annoying when you make a nine-minute argument, pause for an expected reaction, and get: "I'm not sure I followed you" which might as well mean: "I was shampooing my cat and didn't realize I would be called on."

Let's face it, most meetings have always sucked because there's often little to zero accountability for engagement. When we are together in a room, we often compensate with coercive eye contact. Participants feel some obligation to feign interest (even if they're staring at their phones). In situations where you can't demand attention with ocular oppression, you have to learn to do what we should've mastered long ago: *create voluntary engagement.* In other words, you have to create structured opportunities for attendees to engage fully.

There are four broad reasons to hold a meeting: to influence others, to make decisions, to solve problems, or to strengthen relationships. Since all of these are active processes, passive passengers in a meeting rarely do quality work. The precondition for effective meetings — virtual or otherwise — is voluntary engagement.

We've spent the last few years studying virtual training sessions to understand why most virtual gatherings bore groups into a coma. As we've done so, we've discovered and tested five rules that lead to predictably better meeting outcomes. In one study we did, comparing 200 attendees of a face-to-face experience with 200 of a virtual experience, we found that when these rules are applied, 86% of participants report *as high or higher* levels of engagement as in face-to-face meetings. And we've now applied these rules with over 15,000 meeting participants.

Here's what works.

Let's take Raul, a mid-level manager, who is about to lead a 15-minute virtual presentation to 16 of his peers scattered from North to South America. His goal is to convince them they should identify some global sales opportunities from each of their regional account portfolios, then cooperate in pursuing them. To avoid a passive lecture and engage the group, he plans to use 18 slides. Here are the rules Raul should follow.

1. The 60-second rule.

First, never engage a group in solving a problem until they have *felt* the problem. Do something in the first 60 seconds to help them experience it. You might share shocking or provocative statistics, anecdotes, or analogies that dramatize the problem. For example, Raul could share a statistic showing average global deal sizes for a competitor that provokes a sense of inferiority with the group. He could share an anecdote about a frustrated customer who discontinued purchasing because the team failed to offer global pricing and support. Or, he could engage emotions by making an analogy to whales who feed far more effectively when they work together to encircle large schools of krill— and then take turns gorging on the feast. No matter what tactic you use, your goal is to make sure the group empathetically understands the problem (or opportunity) before you try to solve it.

2. The responsibility rule.

When people enter any social setting, they tacitly work to determine their role. For example, when you enter a movie theater, you unconsciously define your role as observer — you are there to be entertained. When you enter the gym, you are an actor — you are there to work out. The biggest engagement threat in virtual meetings is allowing team members to unconsciously take the role of observer. Many already happily defined their role this way when they received the meeting invite. To counteract this implicit decision, create an experience of shared responsibility early on in your presentation. Don't do it by saying, "Okay, I want this to be a conversation, not a presentation. I need all of you to be involved." That rarely works. Instead, create an opportunity for them to take meaningful responsibility. This is best done using the next rule.

3. The nowhere to hide rule.

Research shows that a person appearing to have a heart attack on a subway is less likely to get help the more people there are on the train. Social psychologists refer to this phenomenon as diffusion of responsibility. If everyone is responsible, then no one feels responsible. Avoid this in your meeting by giving people tasks that they can actively engage in so there is nowhere to hide. Define a problem that can be solved quickly, assign people to groups of two or three (max). Give them a medium with which to communicate with one another (video conference, Slack channel, messaging platform, audio breakouts). If you're on a virtual meeting platform that allows for breakout groups, use them liberally. Give them a very limited time frame to take on a highly structured and brief task. For example, three minutes into his pitch, Raul could say something like, "The next slide shows who your partner will be. I want you to take two minutes in your breakout group to identify a global regret: a client you believe you could have had a much bigger deal with if we had worked together better in the past 12 months." Next, he could ask everyone to type their answers into the chat pod, and/or call on one or two to share their example over the phone.

4. The MVP rule.

Nothing disengages a group more reliably than assaulting them with slide after slide of mind-numbing data organized in endless bullet points. It doesn't matter how smart or sophisticated the group is, if your goal is engagement, you must mix facts and stories. We encourage people to determine the *Minimum Viable PowerPoint* (MVP) deck they need. In other words, select the least amount of data you need to inform and engage the group. Don't add a single slide more. A side benefit of this rule is that it forces you to engage the attendees. If you have too many slides, you feel enslaved to "getting through them." If Raul has 18 minutes to get his job done, 15 slides is far too many. He should be able to make his case with one or two slides, then use any additional slides to accomplish the tasks in rules 1-3 above.

5. The 5-minute rule.

Never go longer than 5 minutes without giving the group another problem to solve. Participants are in rooms scattered hither and yon with dozens of tempting distractions. If you don't sustain a continual expectation of meaningful involvement, they will retreat into that alluring observer role, and you'll have to work hard to bring them back. In his 15-minute presentation, Raul should have 2-3 brief, well-defined, and meaningful engagement opportunities. For example, he could wrap up his presentation with a group-generated list of options, then throw out a polling/voting opportunity to determine the team's opinion about where to begin.

The truth is these rules should already be second nature, no matter what kind of meeting you're leading. But the stakes are even higher today when team members are out of sight and their minds are free to wander. Following these five rules will dramatically and immediately change the productivity of any virtual gathering.

Justin Hale is a speaker, training designer, and Master Trainer at VitalSmarts. He has been a lead engineer in designing the VitalSmarts training courses and has facilitated classes and delivered keynote speeches on the skills and principles to 300+ clients and audiences across the world.

Joseph Grenny is a four-time *New York Times* bestselling author, keynote speaker, and leading social scientist for business performance. His work has been translated into 28 languages, is available in 36 countries, and has generated results for 300 of the Fortune 500. He is the cofounder of VitalSmarts, an innovator in corporate training and leadership development.

Harvard Business Review

Communicating Through the Coronavirus Crisis

by Paul A. Argenti

MARCH 13, 2020

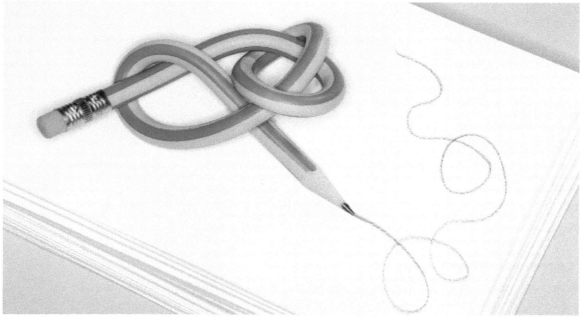

NICHOLAS RIGG/GETTY IMAGES

The coronavirus epidemic seemed far away for me until last week. Then came news reports about someone infected in New Hampshire. Rumors started to spread, closely followed by questions: How can we find out more information? Should we send the kids to school? The next day, we discovered in both the local and national news that the infected person, a resident at our local hospital, had attended a party with students from the Tuck School, where I teach, bringing the crisis right to my office door. Classes and events were canceled and all international travel was suspended for the university. My mind was racing. Should I go in to work? Is it OK to buy lunch here? Are we prepared to quarantine at home? How long will this go on?

In fast-moving and uncertain situations, many leaders face questions they may not even have answers to. As someone who studies crisis communication, I regularly tell my students and clients that you need to communicate early and often with your key constituencies throughout a crisis. Even if you're still trying to understand the extent of the problem, be honest and open to maintain credibility. Approach the situation with empathy. Put yourself in your constituents' shoes to understand their anxiety. You will sometimes get it right, and you will often get it wrong, but it is still better to be as transparent as you can.

Step 1: Create a Team for Centralized Communication

Decentralized communications is understandable and even desirable in large, complex organizations. But in an emergency or fast-moving situation, you need a crisis-response team. With the coronavirus, we are seeing this happening at all levels: President Trump appointed Vice President Pence to head up the national effort. Dartmouth, and many other universities, have created task forces. A school district I worked with this week created a team made up of the superintendent, as well as all of the school principals. Intel has a standing pandemic leadership team in place, as part of its business continuity planning.

Ideally these teams should be small, five to seven people. You need to include a member of the leadership team, someone from corporate communications, an HR executive, and an expert in the area of concern. This team should:

1. Meet regularly to monitor the situation closely as it continues to evolve.
2. Be the main source of information about the crisis.
3. Give regular updates to key constituencies.
4. Be as transparent as possible. Explain what you know, what you don't know, and your sources of information.
5. Be succinct. Long turgid messages written by health professionals or lawyers will not be read or easily understood.

Step 2: Communicate with Employees

Employees are your most important constituency and function as ambassadors to the community. If they aren't informed and don't understand what is going on, communications outside of the organization will be more difficult. The company needs to demystify the situation for employees, put everyone's mind at ease, and provide hope for the future.

Studies have shown that leaders, in particular, have a special role reducing employee anxiety. In my study of crisis communication after 9/11, many employees described how important it was to hear the voice of the leader, whether live or through email, phone messages, or social media. When the coronavirus crisis hit the Tuck School, the MBA program leadership team camped out in a central location to ease everyone's anxiety and provide updates regularly.

To communicate with employees, organizations should:

1. Post information regularly in a highly visible location. This can be a physical location or virtual — email, the company intranet, or a Slack or Facebook channel.
2. Describe how decisions were made about issues such as travel, working from home, etc.
3. Communicate no less than every other day.
4. Try to provide timely information rather than waiting until you know all of the answers.

Step 3: Communicate Regularly with Customers

Customers require a different approach than employees given that companies do not have the same access nor frequency with this constituency. You should:

1. Focus on what is important to the customer. For example, Target sent out a note from the CEO to customers, describing enhanced cleaning procedures and additional staffing for order pickup and drive up services.
2. Provide relief when possible. JetBlue became the first airline to waive change and cancel fees for coronavirus-related concerns. The move went a long way towards reassuring current customers as well as bringing new ones on board. CVS Caremark is working to waive early refill limits on 30-day prescription maintenance medications. Insurance companies, in contrast, do not consider the coronavirus a valid reason for cancelling a flight.
3. Focus on empathy rather than trying to create selling opportunities. Companies should rethink advertising and promotion strategies to be more in line with the current zeitgeist.

Of course, the situation becomes very different when your organization is at the center of a crisis. Many point to the way Johnson & Johnson handled the Tylenol crisis as the gold standard. During the fall of 1982, seven people died after taking Extra Strength Tylenol, which was the best-selling painkiller on the market. Capsules had been injected with cyanide by someone who has never been identified. The company recalled over 30 million bottles of Tylenol, and created new tamper proof packaging.

But Johnson & Johnson also established a set of best practices for communicating in a crisis, including speaking early, often, and directly with its consumers. It issued a national alert, telling people to stop consuming Tylenol products. It established a toll-free number for consumers to call with questions or concerns. It held regular press conferences from company headquarters. Johnson & Johnson leadership, particularly chairman James Burke, took extraordinary steps to communicate with customers and get it right. Many credit his transparency and calm demeanor with stopping the crisis from growing, allowing the company to regain 95% of market share within a few months, and ultimately enhancing the company's reputation.

Step 4: Reassure Shareholders

The epidemic has created intense volatility in the financial markets in the last two weeks and turned what was an incredible bull market into a potential recession. With earnings season just around the corner, publicly listed companies have a special responsibility to communicate the impact of the virus on their operations. Skadden has published considerations related to SEC disclosures, and

Joanne Wong, a senior managing director at FTI Consulting in Hong Kong offers this sound advice for handling investor relations:

1. Be transparent in communicating near-term challenges
2. Use the crisis as an opportunity to reinforce the corporation's long-term fundamentals
3. Communicate what you are doing about the problem

In addition, you should be paying attention to travel guidance and developing communication plans around your annual meeting, including setting up webcasts for shareholders.

Step 5: Be Proactive with Communities

What happens within organizations around the coronavirus affects everyone in the communities around them. At the very least organizations should do their best to make sure their actions do not negatively affect members of the community, but you can also think about a crisis as a time to enhance relationships with the local communities in which you operate by:

1. Providing resources such as cleaning supplies or food for those in quarantine.
2. Providing information to the local media to help to calm the communities down and while also enhancing your organization's credibility.
3. Providing transparency about what is happening within the company rather than going radio silent.

You can also share ways in which you're helping your local, national, or global community in a crisis. For example, as Lauren A. Smith, co-CEO of consulting firm FSG writes, you can use your philanthropic arm to help. Cargill, for example, which has more than 50 business locations and more than 10,000 employees in China, announced a donation of 2 million Yuan to the Chinese Red Cross and sent hundreds of thousands of face masks to affected areas.

When dealing with uncertainty, leaders need to look at communication from the perspective of your audience and have empathy for them rather than fear of doing the wrong thing. This requires companies to communicate when they don't have all of the information, to reveal as much as they can about sensitive information, and to be vigilant about correcting mistakes without worrying about the repercussions. As tennis champion Billie Jean King once said: "Champions keep playing until they get it right."

Paul Argenti is Professor of Corporate Communication at the Tuck School of Business at Dartmouth College.

Harvard Business Review

Slow Down to Make Better Decisions in a Crisis

by Art Markman

MARCH 15, 2020

TALAJ/GETTY IMAGES

The news about the spread of COVID-19 is changing fast — and people are trying to make decisions about everything from whether to cancel vacations to how to best protect themselves and their communities. There are several psychological reasons why you may find decision-making difficult right now.

First, there is a looming present threat. The disease is real. Around the world, people are dying from it and it is spreading rapidly enough that there is new news every day. Humans are wired to pay attention to threats, and so this story captures our attention in a way that a distant threat like climate change does not.

Second, there is a lot of uncertainty about the spread of the virus — how many people have it, how quickly it's moving through communities, how many people will ultimately get it. When it comes to future projections, we're good at understanding linear trends. We are bad at understanding trends that involve an accelerated growth like an exponential function. At the front end of a bloom in a virus, there will be few cases, but they can grow rapidly. The uncertainty that creates for people increases our attention to it.

Third, people have very little control over the spread of the virus. We can engage in actions like washing our hands, avoiding touching our faces, and practicing social distancing, but there are many aspects of the situation that are out of our control. People don't like to be in situations in which they have no agency; it creates additional anxiety as well as a desire to do something to reassert control.

Finally, all of the attempts to control the spread of the virus are fundamentally about prevention. That means that if they are successful, some people will not get sick. Unfortunately, we do not get to run the control condition in which those measures weren't taken. As a result, it is hard to know which actions and programs are having an impact on creating the absence of the disease.

All four of these factors are affecting our behavior and the decisions we make. The threat, uncertainty, and anxiety lead us to make short-sighted decisions.

For example, the uncertainty makes us crave more information so many people are spending a lot of time looking for news updates relating to the virus and its spread. It's good to be informed but we know that the consumption of negative news causes stress and distraction.

Similarly, the lack of agency causes people to seek out actions that will make them feel more in control. Early on, this took the form of buying hand sanitizer and rubbing alcohol. These purchases make some sense, as they can be used to disinfect people and surfaces that might lead to the spread of the virus. But once those stocks dwindled, people still felt like they needed to assert some control, so there was an additional run on toilet paper, paper towels, and bottled water — purchases that make somewhat less sense (and certainly weren't being advised by experts). Still these purchases can temporarily ease some people's anxiety by making them feel like they have done something.

Some people, in the face of anxiety, are making quick decisions about finances as well. With the key stock market indices down roughly 20% in the first few weeks of March, many people are tempted to sell their stocks (and clearly many have). But this is taking a paper loss in the present that is likely to come back in the future (given the way stock markets have acted in the past). People want to take action quickly — even when inaction might be more prudent.

So how do you make good decisions in the face of these psychological factors? The best way to resist the siren call of action is to slow down. Panic makes people want to act right now to avoid a threat, but most of the actions you are likely to take will not be prudent in the face of a potential pandemic.

By slowing down, you can use deliberative reasoning with data — what Keith Stanovich and Richard West called System 2 in their dual-systems approach to the mind — to influence your conclusions. There is a lot of information out there right now about the virus and how to react. Take the time to read and digest it before making important personal and business decisions. There are many actions people should take over the next several weeks and months, but the decision to act should be based on deliberation, sober reflection on data, and discussion with experts — not in reaction to a headline or a tweet.

The same thing holds true for situations that require inaction, when it's better to hold steady and wait for more data. Stanovich and West's System 1 is a fast and intuitive reasoning system that responds to your current motivational state. Those fast judgments are generally biased toward action so you need to slow down to be sure that quick reactions are actually warranted.

All of which is to say that in times of (relatively) slow-developing existential crises like a pandemic, it is best to take your time when making decisions rather than acting on gut feelings. Those quick actions may reduce some of your anxiety in the short-run, but they are likely to create more problems than they solve.

Art Markman, PhD, is the Annabel Irion Worsham Centennial Professor of Psychology and Marketing at the University of Texas at Austin and founding director of the program in the Human Dimensions of Organizations. He has written over 150 scholarly papers on topics including reasoning, decision making, and motivation. His new book is *Bring Your Brain to Work: Using Cognitive Science to Get a Job, Do it Well, and Advance Your Career* (HBR Press).

Harvard Business Review

Build Your Resilience in the Face of a Crisis

by Rasmus Hougaard, Jacqueline Carter and Moses Mohan

MARCH 19, 2020

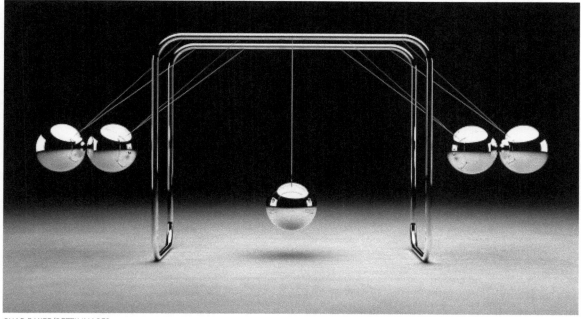

CHAD BAKER/GETTY IMAGES

As the spread and far-reaching impacts of Covid-19 dominate the world news, we have all been witnessing and experiencing the parallel spread of worry, anxiety, and instability. Indeed, in a crisis, our mental state often seems only to exacerbate an already extremely challenging situation, becoming a major obstacle in itself. Why is this and how can we change it? As the CEO of a firm that brings mindfulness to companies to unlock new ways of thinking and working, let me share a bit about how the mind responds to crises, like the threat of a pandemic.

Even without a constant barrage of bad or worrisome news, your mind's natural tendency is to get distracted. Our most recent study found that 58% of employees reported an inability to regulate their attention at work. As the mind wanders, research has shown that it easily gets trapped into patterns and negative thinking. During times of crisis — such as those we are living through now — this tendency is exacerbated, and the mind can become even more hooked by obsessive thinking, as well as feelings of fear and helplessness. It's why we find ourselves reading story after horrible story of quarantined passengers on a cruise ship, even though we've never stepped foot on a cruise ship, nor do we plan to.

When your mind gets stuck in this state, a chain reaction begins. Fear begins to narrow your field of vision, and it becomes harder to see the bigger picture and the positive, creative possibilities in front of you. As perspective shrinks, so too does our tendency to connect with others. Right now, the realities of how the coronavirus spreads can play into our worst fears about others and increase our feelings of isolation, which only adds fuel to our worries.

Watching the past month's turmoil unfold, I have been reminded of the old Buddhist parable of the second arrow. The Buddha once asked a student: "If a person is struck by an arrow, is it painful? If the person is struck by a second arrow, is it even more painful?" He then went on to explain, "In life, we cannot always control the first arrow. However, the second arrow is our reaction to the first. And with this second arrow comes the possibility of choice."

We are all experiencing the first arrow of the coronavirus these days. We are impacted by travel restrictions, plummeting stock prices, supply shortages etc. But the second arrow — anxiety about getting the virus ourselves, worry that our loved ones will get it, worries about financial implications and all the other dark scenarios flooding the news and social media — is to a large extent of our own making. In short, the first arrow causes unavoidable pain, and our resistance to it creates fertile ground for all the second arrows.

It's important to remember that these second arrows — our emotional and psychological response to crises — are natural and very human. But the truth is they often bring us more suffering by narrowing and cluttering our mind and keeping us from seeing clearly the best course of action.

The way to overcome this natural tendency is to build our mental resilience through mindfulness. Mental resilience, especially in challenging times like the present, means managing our minds in a way that increases our ability to face the first arrow and to break the second before it strikes us. Resilience is the skill of noticing our own thoughts, unhooking from the non-constructive ones, and rebalancing quickly. This skill can be nurtured and trained. Here are three effective strategies:

First, calm the mind.

When you focus on calming and clearing your mind, you can pay attention to what is really going on around you and what is coming up within you. You can observe and manage your thoughts and catch them when they start to run away towards doomsday scenarios. You can hold your focus on what you choose (e.g. "Isn't it a gift to be able to work from home!") versus what pulls at you with each ping of a breaking news notification (e.g. "Oh no...the stock market has dropped again.").

This calm and present state is crucial. Right away, it helps keep the mind from wandering and getting hooked, and it reduces the pits of stress and worry that we can easily get stuck in. Even more importantly, the continued practice of unhooking and focusing our minds builds a muscle of resilience that will serve us time and time again. When we practice bringing ourselves back to the present moment, we deepen our capacity to cope and weather all sorts of crises, whether global or personal. (Fortunately, there are a number of free apps available to help calm your mind and increase your own mindfulness.)

Look out the window.

Despair and fear can lead to overreactions. Often, it feels better to be doing something ... anything ... rather than sitting with uncomfortable emotions. In the past few weeks, I have felt disappointment and frustration with important business initiatives that have been adversely impacted by Covid-19. But I have been trying to meet this frustration with reflection versus immediate reaction. I know my mind has needed space to unhook from the swirl of bad news and to settle into a more stable position from which good planning and leadership can emerge. So, I have been trying to work less and to spend more time looking out my window and reflecting. In doing so, I have been able to find clearer answers about how best to move forward, both personally and as a leader.

Connect with others through compassion.

Unfortunately, many of the circles of community that provide support in times of stress are now closed off to us as cities and governments work to contain the spread of the virus. Schools are shut down, events are cancelled, and businesses have enacted work-from-home policies and travel bans. The natural byproduct of this is a growing sense of isolation and separation from the people and groups who can best quell our fears and anxieties.

The present climate of fear can also create stigmas and judgments about who is to blame and who is to be avoided, along with a dark, survivalist "every person for him/herself" mindset and behaviors. We can easily forget our shared vulnerability and interdependence.

But meaningful connection can occur even from the recommended six feet of social distance between you and your neighbor — and it begins with compassion. Compassion is the intention to be of benefit to others and it starts in the mind. Practically speaking, compassion starts by asking yourself one question as you go about your day and connect — virtually and in person — with others: How can I help this person to have a better day?

With that simple question, amazing things begin to happen. The mind expands, the eyes open to who and what is really in front of us, and we see possibilities for ourselves and others that are rich with hope and ripe with opportunity.

Rasmus Hougaard is the founder and managing director of Potential Project, a global leadership and organizational development firm serving Microsoft, Accenture, Cisco and hundreds of other organizations. He is publishing his second book *The Mind of the Leader – How to Lead Yourself, Your People and Your Organization for Extraordinary Results* with HBR Press in March 2018.

Jacqueline Carter is a partner and the North American Director of Potential Project. She is co-author of *The Mind of the Leader – How to Lead Yourself, Your People and Your Organization for Extraordinary Results (HBR Press, 2018)* as well as co-author with Rasmus Hougaard on their first book *One Second Ahead: Enhancing Performance at Work with Mindfulness*.

Moses Mohan is a leadership expert with Potential Project, formerly with McKinsey & Company and former Zen monk.

Harvard Business Review

Don't Hide Bad News in Times of Crisis

by Amy C. Edmondson

MARCH 06, 2020

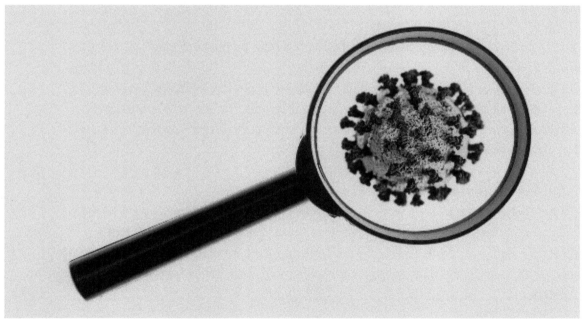

EPOXYDUDE/GETTY IMAGES

If sunshine is the best disinfectant, the opposite is also true: Dark, hidden corners are great places to grow something truly horrible. Few problems improve with age, and public health crises are no exception. Transparency is "job one" for leaders in a crisis. Be clear what you know, what you don't know, and what you're doing to learn more. You can't manage a secret, as the old saying goes.

In recent weeks, I have been wincing at news of China's response to the Covid-19 threat. Back in December there were signs of a dangerous virus. Chinese authorities moved aggressively to hide and to bury the information. The upshot is that six crucial weeks — during which the virus could potentially have been contained — were squandered.

You might say, "Well, that's China for you. Leave transparency to the West." But unfortunately, as numerous articles have reported, the U.S. response is not off to a great start. And history clearly rhymes. This Washington Post article looks back to the response of several western countries to "the Great Influenza" of 1918 and concludes that we are making some of the same mistakes 100 years later. Ironically, the country that was most open about its own flu cases at the time — Spain — suffered reputationally. Its willingness to disclose its data ultimately earned the virus its infamous moniker, the Spanish Flu.

Hiding bad news is virtually a reflex in most organizations, but thoughtful leaders recognize that speaking up early and truthfully is a vital strategy in a fast-moving crisis. Reputation must be seen as a long-term game. Taking the reputational hit today from the release of bad news is likely to earn — for leaders, organizations, and nations alike — dividends in the form of future reputational gain, bringing the benefits that come when internal and external constituents trust what you say and have confidence in your commitment to solving the problems that lie ahead.

Choosing transparency in the midst of any kind of crisis or serious problems requires preparing for what renowned management thinker Peter Senge calls the "worse before better" effect. It's an age-old pattern in complex systems. Organizations that get serious about improvement first must encourage people to speak up honestly about the current problems they see. Without that step, success will be illusory at best. Absent data on what's *not* working, it's all but impossible to know what to fix and how to fix it. No data, no progress.

When the bad news starts pouring in — whether reporting crimes in a city, medical errors in a hospital, or new patient cases in a pandemic — this actually means you've jumped over your first hurdle to success. With accurate information, people can turn their attention and skills to the challenges of developing novel solutions to the newly visible problems. Rather than living with false confidence that all is well, leaders and subject matter experts alike can instead get to work on what needs to be done.

But even though gaining accurate information represents an early success, it can still can be discouraging; the numbers are moving in what surely feels like the wrong direction. We want crime to go down, patients to be safer, and diseases to be wiped out — yesterday! But wishful thinking is not much of a strategy. To make it real, transparency is essential.

Alas, transparency simply will not happen without psychological safety: a climate in which people can raise questions, concerns, and ideas without fear of personal repercussion. After all, who will go out on a limb if that limb is likely to be cut out from under them? This is particularly true in the supercharged atmosphere of a crisis. Absent psychological safety, the higher the stakes of the situation, the greater the risk a person feels they are assuming in speaking up.

In 20 years of studying psychological safety, my colleagues and I have amassed a solid body of evidence that organizations that explicitly value and make paths for speaking up happen are more effective in dealing with challenges of every kind. A handful of case studies in my 2019 book, *The Fearless Organization*, tell compelling stories about the kinds of learning and progress set in motion when problems were placed firmly in bright sunlight — and the catastrophes that ensued when they were not.

It takes courage to choose transparency — and wisdom to know that the choice is the right one for achieving the goals that matter to all. The crucial realization is that if you want others to speak up honestly with what they know, see, and wonder about, it has to start at the top, and in the light.

Amy C. Edmondson is the Novartis Professor of Leadership and Management at Harvard Business School. She is the author of *The Fearless Organization: Creating Psychological Safety in the Workplace for Learning, Innovation, and Growth* (Wiley, 2019) and a coauthor of *Building the Future: Big Teaming for Audacious Innovation* (Berrett-Koehler, 2016).

Harvard Business Review

CRISIS MANAGEMENT

How Bad Times Bring Out the Best in People

by Bill Taylor

MARCH 20, 2020

RYAN MCVAY/GETTY IMAGES

It's easy to look around and see how the Covid-19 crisis has brought out the worst in some people —
from hoarding thousands of bottles of hand sanitizer to crowding bars and restaurants despite public-
health guidelines. But such irresponsible behavior, I believe, is more the exception than the rule.
Time and again, individuals and communities have demonstrated that the worst situations tend to
bring out the best in people and the organizations to which they belong. In every moment of
darkness, it seems, there are countless moments of light — small gestures of compassion and
connection that allow people to show who they are, how they want to live, and what matters to
them.

For her book *A Paradise Built in Hell*, the celebrated nonfiction writer Rebecca Solnit studied impromptu, spontaneous, bottom-up responses to some of the world's worst natural and man-made disasters — deadly earthquakes in San Francisco and Mexico City, the Halifax Explosion of 1917, the September 11 attacks. "The history of disaster," she writes, "demonstrates that most of us are social animals, hungry for connection, as well as for purpose and meaning." A truly dire situation, as tragic as it is, "drags us into emergencies that require we act, and act altruistically, bravely, and with initiative in order to survive or save our neighbors, no matter how we vote or what we do for a living."

As I thought about Solnit's observations, I thought back to an act of business heroism that brought her message to life. It happened during the depths of Hurricane Katrina, which famously ravaged New Orleans, but also devastated the Gulf Coast of Mississippi. For weeks and months, everyday life was a struggle — not just finding food, clothes, or diapers, but finding the money to pay for them. There was no electricity, so no way for credit-card systems to work. Bank branches were flooded and ATM machines were wrecked, so there was no way to get cash.

From this desperate situation emerged an inspired response by employees at Hancock Bank, a community bank based in Gulfport, Mississippi, with roots back to 1899. In the days immediately after Katrina, bank employees, who had their own personal crises to deal with, scavenged the floors, drawers, and bank vaults in the 40 or so Hancock branches that had been obliterated by the storm, along with the waterlogged remains of local casinos. They scooped up all the wet, muddy, filthy cash they could find, and stuffed it into plastic garbage bags. They hooked up washers and dryers to generators, set up rows of ironing boards, and gently cleaned and ironed the cash — they literally laundered money!

They then set up folding tables and tarps outside the branches and distributed cash to anyone who asked for it, even though hardly anyone had an ID, since all of their possessions had been washed away. There were no computer systems, so employees recorded the "withdrawals" on scraps of paper with each person's name, address, and Social Security number. Hancock's makeshift operation distributed more than $42 million in "laundered" cash. As one in-depth news account noted, it was a scene that "would make a mob boss proud."

In reality, this grassroots expression of ingenuity and humanity made the bank and its customers proud. Hancock got back more than 99.5% of the cash it distributed. Its deposits and assets soared: When customers went to a branch to repay the money, or non-customers did the same, they were so grateful that they opened a new account, added to an existing account, and used the bank for their next car loan or mortgage. Hancock CEO George Schloegel told an oral-history project that the attitude was, "You were there when I needed you. You're going to be my bank." In the year after the storm, deposits grew by $1.5 billion.

Meanwhile, Hancock's business strategy was reinforced by these gestures of service and trust. Hancock had always prided itself on a culture of planning for natural disasters, which are part of life in its part of the world. Since Katrina, though, its "last-to-close-first-to-open" philosophy has become core to its brand identity. Ten years after the storm, bank executives were invited to open trading on the Nasdaq stock market to celebrate the region's resilience and the behavior of their employees during the Gulf Coast's "darkest days."

The bottom line: Practical, useful acts of kindness are good for humanity, and good for business. Acts of kindness are also good for the people who do them — and the more tangible the act, the better. Academics who study "prosocial" behavior (as opposed to "antisocial" behavior) often note the power of "helper's high," or what is less charitably called "impure altruism." The satisfaction that comes from doing things for others benefits us as well. "It's hard to do something truly altruistic," argues University of Houston professor Melanie Rudd, "because we always feel good about ourselves after we've performed that act of kindness."

Yes, these are scary, trying, difficult times, and they are likely to get worse before they get better. But as we shake our heads at some bit of reckless behavior featured on the news, or we throw up our hands in despair wondering how our company can make a difference, take a page from Rebecca Solnit's book, and the lessons of Hancock Bank, and look for ways for you and your colleagues to do something to make things a little better.

During the course of her research, Solnit analyzed the work of Charles E. Fritz, a giant of modern disaster studies, a field that emerged after World War II, and she was amazed by his views. Fritz's most "radical premise," she explained, "is that everyday life is already a disaster of sorts, one from which actual disaster liberates us," since it gives each of us the chance to express the best in ourselves. The "merging of individual and societal needs" during a disaster, Fritz argued, "provides a feeling of belonging and a sense of unity rarely achieved under normal circumstances."

So don't be afraid to let bad times bring out the best in your company — and in you.

Bill Taylor is the cofounder of *Fast Company* and the author, most recently, of *Simply Brilliant: How Great Organizations Do Ordinary Things in Extraordinary Ways*. Learn more at williamctaylor.com.

CPSIA information can be obtained
at www.ICGtesting.com
Printed in the USA
JSHW021608220820
7430JS00008B/133

31192022044810

9 781647 820466